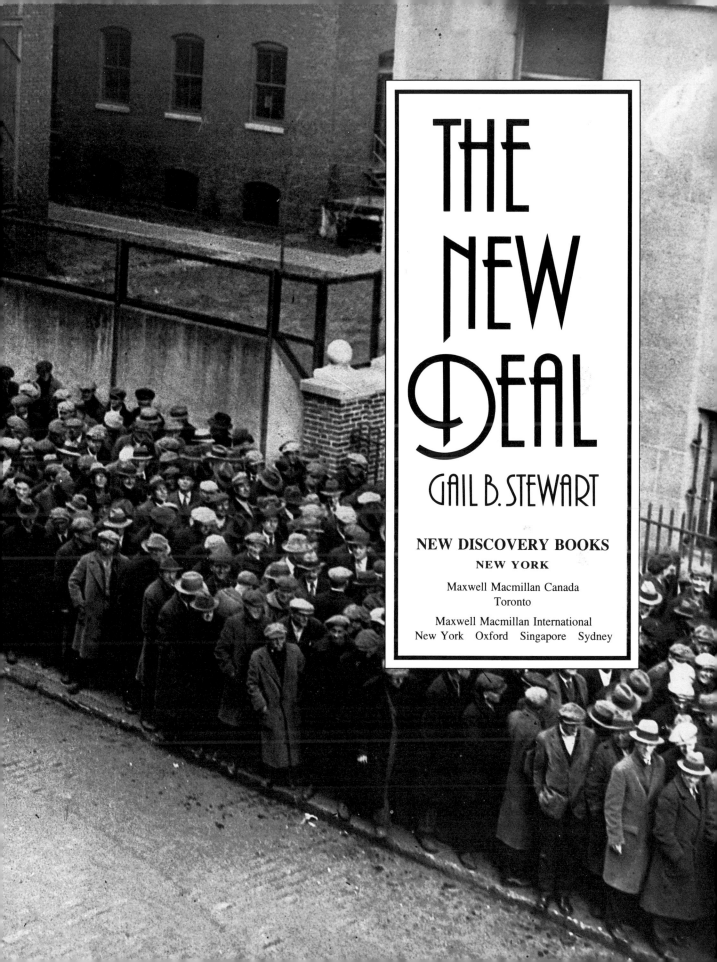

THE NEW DEAL

GAIL B. STEWART

NEW DISCOVERY BOOKS
NEW YORK

Maxwell Macmillan Canada
Toronto

Maxwell Macmillan International
New York   Oxford   Singapore   Sydney

New Discovery Books
Macmillan Publishing Company
866 Third Avenue
New York, NY 10022

Maxwell Macmillan Canada, Inc.
1200 Eglinton Avenue East
Suite 200
Don Mills, Ontario M3C 3N1

Macmillan Publishing Company is part of the
Maxwell Communication Group of Companies.

First edition
Book design by Sylvia Frezzolini
Printed in the United States of America

10 9 8 7 6 5 4 3 2 1

Library of Congress Cataloging-in-Publication Data
Stewart, Gail, 1949–
The New Deal / by Gail B. Stewart.—1st ed.
p.   cm.
''Timestop book.''
Includes bibliographical references and index.
Summary: Discusses the events leading up to America's Great Depression of the 1930s, Roosevelt's rescue of the event with the New Deal, and what caused the ultimate downfall of the New Deal.
ISBN 0–02–788369–8
1. New Deal, 1933–1939—Juvenile literature. 2. United States—History—1933– 1945—Juvenile literature. 3. Depressions—1929—United States—Juvenile literature. [1. New Deal, 1933–1939. 2. United States—History—1933–1945. 3. Depressions—1929.]
I. Title.
E806.S815   1993   92–41264
973.917—dc20

For E. J. Larson and the card-carrying
members of the 1966 "Dicky Hofstadter
for President" campaign

CONTENTS

A ragman rummages through trash cans on New York's Lower East Side searching for food.

"A NEW DEAL FOR THE AMERICAN PEOPLE"

July 1, 1932, was hot and muggy in Chicago. Daytime temperatures were well into the 90s, and evening seemed to bring no relief to the city. Too uncomfortable to be indoors, people sat on stoops outside their homes, fanning themselves with newspapers, talking with their neighbors.

But while most of the city was drowsing in the heat, just west of downtown, at Chicago Stadium, there was frantic activity. Delegates to the Democratic National Convention had reached a consensus the night before. They had chosen the governor of New York, Franklin D. Roosevelt, as their nominee for president. And he was arriving that very night in Chicago to accept his party's nomination.

"I HAVE NO CONTROL OVER THE WINDS OF HEAVEN"

Roosevelt, accompanied by his wife Eleanor, two of his sons, and an array of secretaries and bodyguards, took off from the Albany, New York, airport early that morning in a trimotor airplane known as a "Tin Goose." Despite squalls, strong head winds, and two refueling stops, the plane landed in Chicago at 4:30 that afternoon. Cheering crowds waited for him, both at the airport and along the route to Chicago Stadium.

In-person appearances at political conventions are expected today, but Roosevelt's decision to fly to Chicago that summer was unprecedented. Never before had a nominee appeared at his party's convention—usually a short acceptance speech was given in a press conference in the nominee's home or office.

Governor Roosevelt knew his appearance was dramatic. As he arrived in the convention hall amid the applause and cheers, he apologized for having kept the delegates waiting. "I regret that I am late," he said, "but I have no control over the winds of Heaven."[1]

9

But as for his decision to come to the convention to accept the Democratic nomination, he made no apologies at all. "We will break foolish traditions," he told the delegates, "and leave it to the Republican leadership—far more skilled in that art—to break promises." [2]

HARD TIMES FOR AMERICANS

Americans in 1932 needed no reminders about the Republican leadership. The nation was going through a nightmare that had begun late in 1929. And, although historians say that he was certainly not to blame, most Americans pointed their fingers at the incumbent president, Herbert Hoover.

The nightmare was known as the Great Depression, the worst economic times America has ever seen. It was a time of mass unemployment—up to 80 percent in some industrial cities of the northern states. Millions of homeless people, many of them children, wandered across the country searching for work. Banks were closed, savings were virtually wiped out, and the stock market collapsed.

The lack of money and jobs demoralized people and made them give up hope. The summer before Roosevelt won his party's nomination, a Detroit woman killed her four-year-old son. She told the judge that she couldn't bear watching him go through the agony of starving to death.

A Chicago newspaper reported on the lengths people went to in finding food. "There is not a garbage dump in Chicago which is not diligently haunted by the hungry," the article stated. "Last summer in the hot weather when the smell was sickening and the flies were thick, there were a hundred people a day coming to one of the dumps, falling on the heap of refuse as soon as the truck had pulled out and digging in it with sticks and hands." [3]

"I PLEDGE MYSELF TO A NEW DEAL"

Because Herbert Hoover was the president when the depression began, and because neither he nor the rest of the government could halt it, he was blamed for it. And in the summer of 1932, when the Democrats were meeting to choose a candidate for that November's presidential election, it seemed that people were desperate to hear that the ugliness of the depression could pass.

Roosevelt knew this as he addressed the joyous crowds at Chicago Stadium. As the delegates cheered and waved colorful banners, he spoke to them of a better future, one in which the common people of America would have a chance at prosperity.

"I pledge to you," Roosevelt said solemnly, "I pledge myself to a new deal for the American people. Let us all here assembled constitute ourselves prophets of a new order of competence and ofcourage. This is more than a political campaign; it is a call to arms. Give me your help, not to win votes alone, but to win in this crusade to restore America to its own people."[4]

The reaction to Roosevelt and his call for a "new deal" was widespread celebration. America was in its darkest day, and people were terrified and confused, but Roosevelt was talking about fresh starts and new beginnings. To Americans in that frightening time, the phrase "new deal" symbolized optimism. And if this "new deal" could work, many thought, then maybe there was a chance that the nation could begin its slow climb up from that dark day into the light.

A family of nine in the one-room lean-to they call home in the hills of West Virginia

STAGE · **BROADWAY** · **SCREEN**

VARIETY

PRICE 25¢.

Published Weekly at 154 West 46th St., New York, N. Y., by Variety, Inc. Annual subscription, $10. Single copies, 25 cents.
Entered as second-class matter December 22, 1905, at the Post Office at New York, N. Y., under the act of March 3, 1879.

VOL. XCVII. No. 3   NEW YORK, WEDNESDAY, OCTOBER 30, 1929   88 PAGES

WALL ST. LAYS AN EGG

Going Dumb Is Deadly to Hostess In Her Serious Dance Hall Profesh

A hostess at Roseland has her problems. The paid steppers consider their work a definite profession calling for specialized technique and high-power salesmanship.

"You see, you gotta sell your personality," said one. "Each one of us girls has our own clientele to cater to. It's just like selling dresses in a store—you have to know what to sell each particular customer."

"Home want to dance, some want to kid, some want to get soupy, and others are just 'misunderstood husbands.'"

Girls aspiring for hostess jobs at Roseland must be 21 or older. They must work five nights a week. They are strictly on their own, no salary going with the job and the house collecting 16 cents on every 25 cent ticket. To hold her job, a girl must turn in at least 100 tickets a week during the cold season and 50 in the summer months. In a dull week girls buy their own tickets to keep up the record.

If a partner wishes to sit out a dance, he must pay for the privilege. "Sitting-out time" sells at eight tickets an hour, or $2.25. It's usually a poor sport who will come across with less than $3, many kicking in heavier for a little genial conversation.

The girl who knows her professional dancing trade will keep an alert eye open for potential "glitter-outers," ascertain their hobbies and talk herself into a whole string of tickets. In this way she not only earns money easily, but saves wear and tear on her evening dresses and slippers.

Big money rolls in if she has a good line. One of the most successful girls at Roseland takes this part of her work so seriously that she reads up on current events (sports and stock market included) and has a smattering of current literature and art.

"There are two types of hostesses at Roseland," she said, displaying high brow leanings. "They are the 'mental' and the 'physical.' Surprisingly enough the physical ones are not those who make the most money. One customer will buy three tickets from them at the most. They rely on their sex appeal and go dumb between dances—and that's the surest way to lose a partner, going dumb."

Mental Girls

"The 'mental' girls, being good conversationalists, can wise-crack with the flippant, sympathize with the lonely and know how to salt the fresh boys and make them like it.

Hank on Winchell

When the Walter Winchells moved into 204 West 55th street, late last week, June, that's Mrs. Winchell, selected a special room as Walter's exclusive sleep den for his late hour nights. She chastised the Winchell kiddies when her husband dove in at his usual eight o'clock the first morning.

At noon, Walter's midnight, his sound proof room was banned by so many high C's he awoke with but four hours of dreams and a grouch. Investigated at once, after having signed the lease of course.

Right next door, on the same floor, is the studio of the noted vocal instructor, Kinney. Among his pupils are Ona Munson, Irene Delroy and Marjorie Peterson. They love Winchell like you love carbolic acid.

And Miss Munson is reported to have requested that an amplifier be started hereafter when she runs up the scale.

Demand for Vaude

Springfield, Ill., Oct. 29.

Petitions requesting Publix theatres to resume vaudeville in Decatur, Ill. are in circulation in that city.

Petitions specify that vaudeville at one or more of the three larger Publix houses would furnish employment to a number of Decatur musicians and stage hands and provide larger variety of local entertainment.

Paul Witte, Publix manager in Decatur, states that he believes vaudeville will find a place in Decatur before the season is over.

Pickpocketing Dying Out

Chicago, Oct. 29.

Some 1,000-odd pickpockets who used to make Chicago what it was are no more. A confidential list in the hands of government revenue men shows them to be operating in bottles.

In the last eight months there has not been a complaint or an arrest for pocket picking.

DROP IN STOCKS ROPES SHOWMEN

Many Weep and Call Off Christmas Orders — Legit Shows Hit

MERGERS HALTED

The most dramatic event in the financial history of America is the collapse of the New York Stock Market. The stage was Wall Street, but the onlookers covered the country. Estimates are that 25,000,000 people were in the market at the time.

Tragedy, despair and ruination spell the story of countless thousands of marginal stock traders. Perhaps Manhattan was worst hit in the number of victims. Many may remain broke for the rest of their lives, because the money that disappeared via the ticker tape was the savings of years.

Many people of Broadway are known to have been wiped out. Reports of some in show business losing as much as $300,000 is not hearsay. One caustic comment is that was that the theatre is enough of a gamble without its people to venture into Wall street.

Prominent showmen, several identified with the picture industry *(Continued on page 64)*

FILTHY SHOW OF SHUBERTS GOOD FOR SCREEN

Chicago, Oct. 29.

Shubert's latest musical of their "Night" series, now in Chicago, is so filthy that one of the cast admits embarrassment while in the performance.

The second act of this scramble called "Broadway Nights" is the *(Continued on page 63)*

Soft Drink Smuggling

Kidding Kissers in Talkers Burns Up Fans of Screen's Best Lovers

Talker Crashes Olympus

Paris, Oct. 29.

Fox "Follies" and the Fox Movietone newsreel are running this week in Athens, Greece, the first sound picture heard in the birthplace of world culture, and in all Greece, for that matter.

Several weeks ago, Variety's Cairo correspondent cabled that a cinema had been wired in Alexandria, Cleopatra's home town.

Only Sodom and Gomorrah remain to be heard from.

HOMELY WOMEN SCARCE; CAN'T EARN OVER $25

No homely ones on Broadway! And now it looks as if Crosby Gaige may have to postpone production of "One Beautiful Evening" because the Main Stem is devoid of the non-beauts necessary for the casting of the show.

Arthur Lubin, caster for the producer, for several weeks has been trying to land the right type of women. A most unusual piece, the drama has an all-women lineup, and, although as many as 28 are needed, all must be homely—and middle age or over, except for two who can be young.

Vera Caspary wrote the play and it centers about conditions at a club for girls where requirements of residence demand that the girls must not earn over $25 per week in order to live under its roof. That's why they must be homely.

Ads for Execs

Chicago, Oct. 29.

Newspaper ad calling for potential executives for the Publix-B. & K. organization here, drew heavy response, with over 100 applicants.

From all walks of life, with several $20,000-a-year men among the mob, seeking a chance to break into the show business.

Boys who used to whistle and girls who used to giggle when love scenes were flashed on the screen are in action again. A couple of years ago they began to take the love stuff seriously and desisted but the talkers are reviving the ha ha for film osculators.

Heavy loving lovers of silent picture days accustomed to charming audiences into spasms of silent ecstasy when kissing the leading lady are getting the bird instead of the heartbeat. The sound accompaniment is making it tough.

Such a picture romancer as John Gilbert is getting laughs in place of the sighs of other days, and the flaps who still think he's grand are getting sore. One little flap had to be quieted by an usher when making a commotion during a Gilbert picture at the Capitol, New York. The person sitting next to her, like many others in the house, took Gilbert's passion lightly. The girl jumped to his defense and started to bawl out the talker derider.

Not only has Gilbert received the bird lately, but all of the other male screen players who specialize in romance. Charley Farrell in "Sunny Side Up" draws many a giggle from his mush stuff.

In the silents when a lover would whisper like a ventriloquist, lips apart and unmoved and roll his eyes passionately preparatory to the clinch and then kiss, it looked pretty natural and was believable. The build-up to the kissing now makes a gag of the kiss.

When the kiss is with serious intent, the laughs are out of order. It's burning the impressed female fans to see their favorite kissers kidded when kissing.

In Reverse

Seems the only type of love stuff received as intended since advent of the talkers in the comedy love scene. The screen comics are becoming the heavy lovers and the heavy lovers comedians.

The normal kiss, delivered with the usual smack, sounds like an explosion. For that reason clinch scenes in the early talkers had them rolling in the aisles.

Toning down their kissing to make it noiseless has made bum kissers of the screen's best lovers, but, audible or silent, the kisses are getting laughs that don't belong.

Hollywood, Oct. 29.

Soft pedal on dialog in romantic love scenes in the future. Here.

The front page of the show-business newspaper Variety *reflects the condition of the country after the 1929 stock market crash.*

CHAPTER ONE

AMERICA ON EASY STREET

The Democrats in 1932 brimmed with confidence. They were certain that Roosevelt would win the election in November. Roosevelt's running mate, John Nance Garner, advised him after the convention, ''All you have to do to win is stay alive.''[1]

Yet historians say that just a few years before, the Republican party under Herbert Hoover seemed rock solid. The economy was strong, employment was high, and business was humming. The Republicans had been so successful, in fact, that political analysts of the day speculated that the Democrats were all but dead and buried.

How did things change so quickly? How could a nation plunge from prosperity to economic tragedy in so short a time? Without answering these questions, Roosevelt and his ''new deal'' promises are difficult to understand.

LOOKING INWARD

Although the Great Depression began in 1929, the roots of the trouble go back earlier, to the end of World War I. The war had been a costly one for America, both in terms of money and human life. The United States spent more than $30 billion in the war, and the country had seen thousands of its young men killed in the brutal trench warfare.

Because the war had been so costly, there was a great political backlash against President Woodrow Wilson and his Democratic party. After the war, Americans blamed Wilson for having dragged them into it. When Warren G. Harding, a Republican, ran for president in 1920 promising a ''return to normalcy,'' he was elected hands down.

''Normalcy'' meant that the United States would embrace a policy of *isola-*

tionism—thinking more nationally and less globally. No longer would Americans become involved in the world's problems—it made more sense to concentrate on their own. And no longer would American companies seek world markets for their products. Instead, tariffs were enacted that would discourage foreign businesses from selling products in the United States that might compete with American-made goods.

AN EASY TRANSITION

Business and industry had become stronger during the war. Factories had been operating nonstop, turning out tanks, airplanes, rifles, and clothing for the soldiers overseas. The years in which the United States fought in the war saw a mass migration of workers from the farms of rural America to the cities. Workers were

---

DARK SHADOWS THREATEN AMERICA'S PROSPERITY

Even though the world seemed prosperous and rosy to Americans in the 1920s, there were ominous signs that all was not well. In Europe, especially, there were economic problems that would grow and worsen and that would affect the good times Americans were experiencing. The worst of these economic dark shadows loomed in Germany.

After World War I ended, Germany had no choice but to sign the Treaty of Versailles, which had imposed a large number of restrictions that the Germans felt were terribly unfair. In addition to limiting Germany's armed forces and taking away some of its territory, the Allies (primarily Great Britain and France) ordered Germany to pay large sums of money in reparations to the nations it had attacked.

Germany after World War I was not strong. Its factories and businesses no longer operated. Because of this, it was difficult for the country to make regular payments on the billions of dollars it owed as reparations. The German economy was in a shambles.

Because the nations of Europe are trading partners and rely on one another economically, Germany's financial woes affected France, England, and other American trading partners. It did not take long, then, for the economic depression that gripped Europe in the 1920s to intensify the hardships that had begun in America.

desperately needed to fill the factories; employment figures were at an all-time high.

But the need for mass production did not lessen after the war. People were eager to buy radios, refrigerators, and electric washing machines. And the factories, still geared up for a high rate of production, made the easy transition to peacetime industry. With the demand for such goods high, people who wanted jobs had little trouble getting them. And because so many people were working, there were lots of people with money to spend. The cycle of earning and spending continued.

Although business as a whole was booming in the years after World War I, there was no industry that grew as fast as the automobile industry, still in its infancy in the 1920s. Glass, steel, oil, and gasoline were needed, as well as paved roads, and these needs meant more jobs for American workers. The demand for Model Ts skyrocketed—the number of cars on American roads soared from 7 million in 1919 to 23 million in 1923.

It seemed that by turning its back to the rest of the world and concentrating on itself, America was rapidly becoming stronger. People were more confident. As one historian writes, "With industry booming and most of America employed, a feeling of great optimism swept the country. The 'American dream' seemed to be working."[2]

A HIGH REGARD FOR BUSINESS

Before World War I there had been some serious talk of putting stricter controls on big business in America. Scandals, unfair labor practices, and other improper behavior had been reported, and there were many in Congress who had wanted the government to become more closely involved with how businesses were run.

But the war and its aftermath had changed all that. Hadn't industry swung into high gear to produce weapons and war material when the country needed it most? Few could find fault with the way American industry had contributed toward the war effort. Efficient, quality production had continued, too, to meet the rising demands of Americans for the products they wanted. By the 1920s the reputation of business was golden.

Calvin Coolidge, who took over the presidency after Harding died, felt that business was what the strength of America was built upon. "The business of America is business," Coolidge said in 1924. "The man who builds a factory builds a temple; the man who works there worships there."[3]

If there were warning signs during Coolidge's term of office that the economy was in for trouble, he did not heed them. "If you see ten troubles coming down the road," Coolidge once explained, "you can be sure that nine will run into the ditch before they reach you."[4] Historians say that Coolidge's "don't go looking for problems" attitude was typical of the 1920s. Business was booming, the economy seemed strong, people were confident. Confident, in fact, almost to the point of feeling invincible.

SPEND, BORROW, AND SPEND SOME MORE

In 1928 Coolidge decided not to run for a second term. His secretary of commerce, Herbert Hoover, was elected to the presidency. Hoover shared his predecessors' views on the economy, and American business continued on its upward spiral.

"We have not yet reached the goal, but given a chance to go forward with the policies of the last eight years," said Hoover in a 1929 speech, "we shall soon, with the help of God, be within sight of the day when poverty will be banished from the nation."[5]

And the way to eliminate poverty, if one could believe the current wisdom, was to spend money, not save it. Advertisers were assuring American families that it was foolish to tighten their belts, that the more they spent the more prosperous they'd be. People were assured that economist Simon Patten was absolutely right when he said, "I tell my students to spend all they have and borrow more and spend that. It is foolish for persons to scrimp and save."[6]

It seemed, in the late 1920s, that Americans were taking Patten's advice. Spending money was fashionable, and the biggest spenders were the most admired. In January 1929 *Time* magazine's Man of the Year was Walter Chrysler. He had just introduced two new cars, the Plymouth and the luxurious DeSoto. In addition, he was building a gigantic new skyscraper in New York. To the American public, Chrysler was the embodiment of prosperity and strength.

A NEW KIND OF SPENDING

One sure sign of prosperity was to own things—automobiles, big houses, fancy appliances. But what about the people who did not have money for such products? For these people there came a new phenomenon that allowed almost anyone to be a consumer. It was called "installment buying."

The premise for installment buying was simple. A consumer could buy products on credit. By putting a few dollars down and arranging to make regular payments each month, one could buy a new automobile, an electric washing machine, or an expensive coat. "A dollar down and a dollar when they catch you" became a common saying of the times.

The system was extraordinarily popular. Consumers liked it because it allowed them to own expensive things immediately, instead of after years of saving. Store owners liked the system because it moved merchandise quickly, leaving space for new products. And industry liked it because more consumers were buying their products, creating a demand for their factories to turn out more.

Installment buying became the rule rather than the exception as time went by. By 1928 eight out of every ten cars in the United States were bought on credit. "Coming from a rather poor family, I liked the setup," remembers Sam Johnson, a Minnesotan who was a young man in the 1920s. "I could have my new Ford sitting outside the house the very day I wanted it. People could buy a used one for ten dollars, but I wanted a new one. Now, the people on the next block paid cash for theirs, I'm sure of it. But mine was just as shiny, and the motor worked just as good. For all those people knew, I'd paid for mine same as they did."[7]

PLAYING THE MARKET

The stock market was another way Americans could take advantage of installment buying. For years, businesses had depended on the stock market as a way to raise money. Instead of borrowing money from a bank, they offered stock in their companies to any investor who could come up with the cash. Each share of stock became more valuable, and *dividends,* another word for interest, were paid regularly to the investor, the amount depending on how successful the business had become.

During the administration of Calvin Coolidge, stock market activity had increased greatly. Even though the stock market had always been risky—for of course one could lose his or her money if the business failed—there was a growing confidence that no business could possibly lose money.

Investors pumped millions of dollars into stocks, driving the price of shares higher and higher. Businesses were being injected with all the money they needed, and so their stocks paid high dividends, enticing more people to "play the market."

By the late 1920s, Americans were able to buy stocks the same way they were buying their automobiles—on installment. Stockbrokers, who did the actual buying and selling of stocks for their clients, allowed customers to pay 10 or 15 percent down on stock. This was called "buying on margin." The broker would loan the rest to his client, receiving the balance of his money when the stock increased in value.

LITTLE CASH, BIG HOPES

Playing the stock market soon became the most popular activity in America. Everyone who had a few dollars saved wanted a chance to get rich overnight. Newspapers and magazines were full of "get rich quick" stories—common, ordinary people who had become millionaires overnight by buying the right stock.

The number of stockbrokers in America grew—from fewer than 30,000 in 1920 to more than 70,000 by 1929. Originally confined to plush offices in the nicest parts of the largest cities, the brokers now had offices in every town and village in America. Many set up tiny offices near college campuses and in the poorer sections of town, too, for their clients came from all walks of life.

"Shoe-shine boys were buying $100 worth of stock for $8 and $10," reports Anne Schraff in her book *The Great Depression and the New Deal*. "Stocks were rising in value so fast that 'becoming as rich as Rockefeller' seemed within the grasp of ordinary people. Teenage typists and stenographers, small shopkeepers, and the retired joined the mad buying spree." [8]

It was as if Americans felt that they had a duty to become wealthy. Indeed, those who did not choose to risk money in the stock market were looked upon almost with disdain. Money was there to be made, it seemed, and if one followed a few basic rules, it was childishly simple.

"If a man saves $15 a week and invests in good common stocks," advised John Raskob, Democratic party chairman in the summer of 1929, "and allows the dividends and rights to accumulate, at the end of 20 years he will have at least $80,000 and an income from investments of around $400 a month. He will be rich. And because income can do that, I am firm in my belief that anyone not only can be rich, but ought to be rich." [9]

WARNING SIGNS

Stock prices continued to skyrocket late in 1929, climbing to record heights each week. On the surface this seemed to indicate continued prosperity and growth, but

THE FLORIDA LAND BOOM

Besides investing in the stock market in the 1920s, Americans bought land. The idea was to purchase property, then sell it to someone else for a profit. And just as prices in the stock market continued to rise during this time, land prices were skyrocketing.

The prime location between 1924 and 1926 was Florida. With its warm, sunny climate, Florida seemed ideal. Besides, with the coming of the automobile, Americans were traveling more than ever before. It seemed logical, at least to many, that real estate there would be a foolproof way of making lots of money.

More than 90 percent of the people who bought Florida land had no intention of living there themselves. On the contrary, their idea was to turn around and sell it again. Much of the land was lovely, although there were some parcels of land that were no more than swampland, far from the sandy beaches in the travel photos. Even so, it passed from buyer to buyer, increasing in price each time.

But the game had to end, and most investors knew it. However, as historian Robert McElvaine writes in *The Great Depression,* the trick was "to ride with the expansion as long as possible and get out before the collapse."

The collapse came with fury, in the form of two violent hurricanes that destroyed a great deal of land in 1926 and 1928. Land that had once seemed like a fine investment became worthless. After that, the speculation in Florida land never revived.

some economists were concerned. Prices had been driven so high, and there was so much investment, that there was nowhere for things to go but downhill.

Especially troubling to experts was the fact that there were so many brokers who had overextended themselves. Record numbers of investors buying on margin had forced brokers to put up large percentages of the money to buy stocks. The stockbrokers were short of cash, so they had borrowed from banks, which were now heavily into debt.

Economists did have one way of controlling the amount of money circulating among banks and stockbrokers. It was the Federal Reserve Board, or Fed, as it is often called. The Fed controls the amount of money in the American economy. It lends money to banks at a rate of interest, just as banks lend money to their customers at a given rate of interest. It is the Fed that determines the rate, for banks and other lending institutions charge their customers the same interest that they themselves are charged.

When interest rates are high, it becomes more difficult to borrow large sums of money, because it is so expensive to pay it back. Economists concerned about the furious activity on the stock market decided early in 1927 to use the Fed to cut down on the numbers of stocks bought on margin. They raised the Fed's interest rates. However, there was almost no effect reflected in the market.

In a bolder move later, the Fed declared that money it lent to banks could not be used for investment in the stock market. This ploy seemed to work for a month or so, but eventually prices rose and the upward spiral continued as before.

SELL!

Prices began to drop in the stock market in September 1929. The drop continued all during that month and into October, though many people refused to become alarmed. There had been times before when prices had dropped, but they had always bounced back. However, that was not the case on October 24, known as Black Thursday.

Prices on the stock exchange began dropping crazily all morning. By 11:00 A.M. the plunge was out of control, and the brokers on the floor of the New York Stock Exchange (the nation's largest) were in a state of panic. Anne Schraff describes them as "milling, screaming men, their faces alabaster white with fear." [10]

Prices of what had been good, reliable stocks were half of what they had been the day before. And other investors, noting the plunge, were afraid to sit on their own shares. After all, they thought, by tomorrow the price might be one-fourth of what it had been. They, too, called their brokers and told them to sell. Soon 13 million shares of stock had changed hands.

A reporter from the *New York Times* was present at the New York Stock Exchange that day, and described the terrified investors—thousands of them—throwing their holdings "into the whirling Stock Exchange pit for what they would bring. Losses were tremendous and thousands of prosperous brokerage and bank accounts, sound and healthy a week ago, were completely wrecked in the strange debacle. . . . Wild-eyed speculators crowded the brokerage offices, awed by the disaster which had overtaken many of them." [11]

Clerks on Wall Street work into the midnight hours in the aftermath of the crash.

Two interested investors follow the rise and fall of stock values on the board of the New York exchange.

Market in Panic as Stocks Are Dumped in 12,894,600 Share Day; Bankers Halt It

Outside J. P. Morgan & Co.'s

A newspaper headline the day after Black Thursday

Worried customers gather outside the stock exchange in New York after hearing news of the crash.

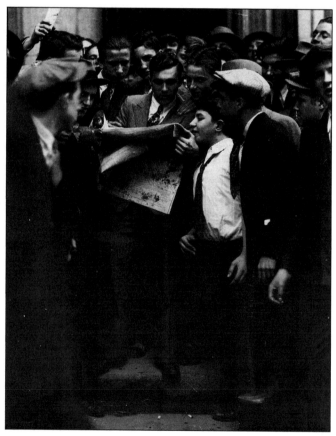

Brokers anxiously scan ticker-tape printouts after the crash, when stock prices rose briefly.

Mounted police try to keep order outside the New York Stock Exchange.

As news of the crash traveled, people flocked into Wall Street trying to find out what had become of their money.

HELP, BUT TO NO AVAIL

Worried about how so much selling would affect them, some of the nation's most influential bankers hurriedly met that Thursday. They decided to pool $40 million from their banks and buy stock, trying to drive the price up and calm people's fears.

The gamble seemed at first as though it would pay off. By the end of Thursday, and again on Friday and Saturday, the market seemed to settle down. However, the following Monday the plunge began again, and this time nothing could stop it.

But Tuesday, October 29, stocks were virtually worthless. On Wall Street, the center for financial activity in New York, there was hysteria, weeping, and even reports of mass suicides among bankers, brokers, and investors. That day, more than 16 million shares of stock were sold. They were put on the market, but no one was buying at any price. Whole fortunes were lost—people who had been among America's richest investors became paupers overnight.

Like ripples in a pond, the effects of the crash of the stock market moved outward to include almost every American, investor or not. The Great Depression had begun, and it seemed to be beyond anyone's control.

An apple seller stands beside a sign asking for help in locating his missing wife.

CHAPTER TWO

HARD TIMES

Economists call what happened in America in late October 1929 as a "panic." Plummeting prices in the stock market caused many investors to become frightened and sell their stock, and that caused stock prices to drop even more.

There had been panics several times before, and the American economy had weathered them. There was no way for people to know, late in 1929, that this latest panic was the beginning of a depression that almost sent the nation into collapse.

"BUSINESS IS SOUND"

The reaction of President Hoover was one of denial. No problem existed, he said, and anyone who felt otherwise was greatly mistaken. In a speech given October 25, the day after the initial stock market crash, Hoover insisted, "The traditional business of the country, that is, the production and distribution of commodities, is on a sound and prosperous basis."[1]

Bankers, stockbrokers, and industrial leaders wanted to believe that he was right. Without confidence in business, people would not invest, and the economy could not get along without investors. Americans were urged to think positively and not to curtail their buying because of a "momentary" setback in the stock market.

The chairman of the board of Bethlehem Steel, Charles Schwab, reassured Americans that by reinvesting money they would be doing the smartest thing for their country. "Never before," he said, "has American business been as firmly entrenched for prosperity as it is today."[2]

Jimmy Walker, the popular mayor of New York City, urged theaters to book only upbeat, happy movies, to lift people's spirits. And everywhere people could see billboards put up by the National Association of Manufacturers with beautiful, smiling women assuring them, ''Business is good. Keep it good. Nothing can stop U.S.''

"WHAT HAVE WE DONE?"

But business was *not* good, and most Americans knew it. Although the average American had not been a heavy investor in the stock market, it did not take long for the effects of the crash to be felt by everyone.

The banks were very short of cash. As a direct result of the stock market crash, the large loans to investors and brokers buying on margin could not be repaid. The repayment of loans is one way banks keep replenishing their supply of cash. Deposits are another. But as bank customers learned that their banks were running short of money, there was a mad scramble to withdraw money. Soon there was none left to be withdrawn, and banks were forced to close their doors. Late in 1929 and into 1930 they were closing at the rate of 50 or 60 each day.

''I saw my father cry, and I had never seen him show emotion like that before,'' remembers one man who was seven years old when the stock market crashed. ''He and my mother had saved almost $400—we were not rich people—and it was our life savings. We walked to the bank and stood in a line with lots of other people. They were angry, talking about how this kind of thing should not be happening in the United States of America, banks taking money and not giving it back.

''Pretty soon the line wasn't moving any more, and everyone started shouting and waving their fists. We walked closer to the building and there was a sign that said CLOSED UNTIL FURTHER NOTICE. My father said he knew what that meant, that we'd never see that $400 again. He started to cry. ''Chester, what have we done, what have we done?'' he kept saying.[3]

"HAPPY DAYS ARE HERE AGAIN"

Just a few weeks after the crash, $30 billion had simply vanished. Life savings in banks and financial investments in what were thought to be dependable stocks had blown away.

The failing of many of the nation's banks frightened Americans. And although businesses and economists were urging them to buy and invest, they didn't. They saved what money they could—in sugar bowls and inside mattresses, rather than in the struggling banks. And instead of buying washing machines, automobiles, and new clothes, more and more people chose to get along with what they had.

Frantic customers wait outside a bank that has been taken over by the federal government waiting for news of their investments.

This "save rather than spend" attitude began a new cycle. Companies that had been turning out record numbers of products now had no one to sell them to. Instead, they laid off employees. By April 1930 there were three million Americans who had lost their jobs. And without jobs, people could not hope to buy more than just the basic necessities. This caused even more businesses to close, and more employees to be laid off.

President Hoover continued to issue optimistic statements about the economy. In the spring of 1930 he said, "We have now passed the worst, and we shall rapidly recover."[4] As if to reinforce Hoover's cheerful ideas, a new song called "Happy Days Are Here Again" was getting lots of play on the radio. But even though the song promised a return to more prosperous times, Americans weren't buying it. There was nothing but trouble in their lives, and it showed no signs of lessening.

A group of unemployed men gather around a potbellied stove at a mission.

BELT-TIGHTENING

The depression forced many Americans to change the whole order of their lives. Where they lived, what they ate, whether or not they worked, and how they spent their money—all of these things were affected by the unraveling economy.

It is important to remember that in those days there was no such thing as government-run unemployment insurance or Social Security payments. People who fell upon hard times had to get along the best they could; if things were really bad, they had to turn to friends or family for help, or to a private charity.

The family structure was drastically affected. Since unemployment was so high, it naturally followed that millions of families could not afford to pay the rent as they had previously. As a solution, there was a great deal of "doubling up"—two families crowding into one apartment and splitting the rent. Many young families chose to do their doubling up with one set of parents. In her book *The Great Depression and the New Deal*, Anne Schraff writes of one Italian family whose ''doubling up'' resulted in the return of all ten children with their spouses and children—all under one roof!

Often the crowding and lack of privacy caused trouble in families. However, having an extended family all together was handy, for the grandmothers could teach the younger ones ways to save money. Knowledge that only a few years before might have seemed silly and old-fashioned became highly useful, as young

---

MR. GLAD TO THE RESCUE!

Hard times saw crowds of out-of-luck people waiting outside employment offices or church-run soup kitchens, especially in the early years of the depression. In New York City, hard times also brought a variety of interesting characters to offer their version of how the depression could be solved.

One of the most visible was an anonymous friend of the poor who called himself Mr. Glad. He visited Times Square in New York City often, handing out nickels, warm gloves, sandwiches, coffee, and fruit. Mr. Glad was also a firm believer in number theories. He distributed little cards, pointing out that the sum of the digits of the depression year 1930 was 13. This was true, he claimed, for other years in which the United States had suffered little depressions, such as 1903, 1912, and 1921. He had no real economic solution, only reminding people that if his theory was correct, there would be no further depressions until the year 2027.

Mr. Zero was another visitor to Times Square in 1930. Like Mr. Glad, Mr. Zero spent hundreds of dollars purchasing doughnuts and cakes to give away to the hungry in New York City. But unlike his counterpart, Mr. Zero had a plan that he felt would solve both hunger and unemployment. He proposed that homeless New Yorkers be auctioned off to wheat farmers in Kansas who needed farmhands.

In exchange, the farmers would donate wheat that Mr. Zero would bake into bread for the poor. As writer Robert Bendinernotes in his book *Just Around the Corner*, ''Nothing came of it, though some Kansas wheat men were ready to offer $1.50 a day for labor, plus room and board.''

A sign of the times: A victim of the stock market crash tries to come up with some cash.

families learned how to make their own soap, to cure and smoke meats, to bake their own bread, to sew and quilt, and to can preserves. Historians say the makers of glass jars were one of the few industries whose business soared during the depression—in 1931 they recorded their highest sales in 11 years.

Most families had to pay very close attention to how every penny was spent. When the family automobile broke down, it was simply hauled into the garage and its owners rode bicycles or walked. Restaurants noted a drastic drop—almost 65 percent—in their business between 1929 and 1933; people simply couldn't afford to eat out. Even at home, meat became a once-a-week luxury, even though the price of hamburger had dropped to 15 cents a pound in 1931. And because electric bills were often too much for families to pay, many Americans returned to kerosene lamps.

Sometimes this belt-tightening had negative effects. People put off receiving medical help, often until a disease had become uncontrollable. Dentists complained that most of their work during the depression was pulling teeth that could have been saved if the patients had been seen on a regular basis.

But more important, people tended to lose their sense of hope for the future as the depression continued into its second year with no end in sight. The birth rate dropped, for young married couples had no wish to bring children into such a bleak, gray world.

DEPRESSION PSYCHOLOGY

Unemployment brought some very obvious changes—such as hunger, poverty, and homelessness—to American families. But there were other, more subtle changes that affected families, too, and these were often just as harmful.

America was a society in which men were *expected* to work, to be successful. Joblessness had always been considered a result of laziness. If a man did not work, he was believed to be lacking in drive, ambition, or ability. That is why, when millions of men were suddenly, through no fault of their own, out of work, they felt ashamed.

Many would hide the fact that they no longer had jobs to go to—getting dressed in suits and ties and waiting for the same train to take them into the city. Keeping up was very important to many American families.

While some kept up a brave, false front, other families seemed almost to disappear—shunning friends and neighbors to avoid revealing that they had fallen on hard times. As Dixon Wecter writes in *The Age of the Great Depression,* "Jobless men and their families often kept to themselves—shabbily dressed children hiding from visitors, adults sullenly refusing hospitality from still employed friends because of the hardship of repaying an evening at cards over sandwiches and coffee."

HOOVERVILLES AND MAKE-BELIEVE SOUP

While doubling up was a strain on families, there were millions who were far worse off. These were people who could not pay rent and whose jobs had vanished. With no means of support, and chances of employment dimmer by the day, these people became part of the growing number of homeless in depression America.

Many of the homeless were people who had been poor before, but for a great many of them, life on the streets was a new and frightening experience. Writer Sherwood Anderson wrote about them, ''men who are heads of families creeping through the streets of American cities, eating from garbage cans; men turned out of houses and sleeping week after week on park benches, on the ground in parks, in the mud under bridges. . . . Our streets are filled with beggars, with men new to the art of begging.''[5]

During the early years of the depression, miniature ''communities'' of these people sprouted up around towns and cities, usually under bridges or near a river. Sarcastically called Hoovervilles after the man people held responsible for the depression, they were collections of homes made of packing crates, scrap iron, and anything else that might be useful to keep the rain and cold out. Sometimes an old automobile seat taken from a dump served as a bed.

One historian recalled passing such a community in New York City. ''Along the Hudson, below Riverside Drive, I daily passed the tar paper huts of a Hooverville where scores of families lived the lives of reluctant gypsies, cooking whatever they had to cook over open fires within sight of passengers on the double deck Fifth Avenue buses.''[6]

Another described the shacks of a Hooverville as ''the size of a dog house or chicken coop, often constructed with much ingenuity out of wooden boxes, metal cans, strips of cardboard, or old tar paper. Here human beings lived on the margin of civilization by foraging for garbage, junk, and waste lumber.''[7]

Some Hooverville residents panhandled for food money; for millions, though, the breadline was the only source of food. Soup kitchens, funded and staffed by the Salvation Army, political groups, or churches, opened in cities and towns around the United States. In New York City, for instance, 80 of these breadlines served about 100,000 free meals each day in 1930.

The fare was not fancy—often a plate of beans or rice and some watered-down coffee were offered. However, the most common item served was what many of the poor called ''make-believe soup''—make-believe because it was so thin.

Unemployed men living in a makeshift dugout in New York's Central Park

"Jungle City," the group of shacks located in the drained reservoir of Central Park where many of New York's homeless families lived

A line of unemployed outside a public assistance office

Depression-era actresses Ethelind Terry, Marion Marchante, and Armida help to distribute food to out-of-work men.

Breadlines were long—often a quarter mile—and those at the head of the line usually got mostly water. Those at the line's end usually were luckier, getting a bit of potato or fatty meat from the bottom of the pot.

ON THE MOVE

There was even a class of poor people below the Hooverville dwellers. These were transients, the ones who drifted aimlessly from city to town. They slept in barns or in farmers' fields and often stole food along the way. Historians estimate that there were more than two million drifters during the depression. More than 250,000 of these were children. Girls often disguised themselves as boys to avoid sexual assaults.

Most of these homeless people traveled by railroad. Trains have always been used by drifters, who are often called hoboes. In fact, the Missouri Pacific Railroad estimated that there were 14,000 hoboes using their trains in the summer of 1929. However, by the summer of 1931, that number had jumped to 185,000. And by 1933, the railroad estimated that a million people were riding the rails.

Previously, railroad officials had hired security men to evict transients from the trains. But during the depression, railroads realized they couldn't control the growing numbers; in fact, some companies even added a couple of extra cars on their trains to accommodate the homeless.

THE RULES HAVE CHANGED

As the depression continued, it became increasingly clear that many old ideas just didn't hold true any longer. "People had grown up believing that if you worked hard, kept your nose to the grindstone, and did your duty, things would work out," writes Schraff. "Only loafers and those of low moral character found themselves jobless and homeless. But somehow all the rules had been changed."[8]

The rules *had* changed, for in the United States of America, people were actually starving to death. Record numbers of people were being treated in hospitals for severe malnutrition. In communities that saw great numbers of unemployed and homeless people, there were often sensible solutions. Many such communities had, by 1932, turned over tracts of public land to the poor for cultivation. In Gary, Indiana, for instance, 20,000 families raised their own fruits and vegetables on city-owned land.

"It was land that wasn't used for much anyway," remembers a man from

Cincinnati, Ohio. "Why not let people have the dignity of growing their food, rather than being humiliated every day by asking for handouts?"[9]

DESPERATE FOR WORK

As the depression wore on, unemployment figures skyrocketed. In 1930, four million employable people were out of work; by the spring of 1931 that figure had doubled. And by December the nation's unemployment figure was a staggering 13.6 million—a third of the labor force.

Women and minorities in unskilled labor positions were the first to be fired. According to one historian, these were "the shock troops, followed by white collar workers and technicians. Professional classes felt the jar a little later, as teachers' and ministers' salaries were cut or fell into arrears."[10]

During the depression, workers were happy to take a pay cut—usually at least 10 percent—for the alternative was to not have a job at all. But the resulting wages were shamefully low, especially for unskilled labor. A survey of working women in Chicago in 1931, for instance, showed that many were working for less than 25 cents per hour; a fourth of the women surveyed made less than 10 cents per hour. One woman in New York made 23 cents for every 200 pants pockets she sewed!

Somewhere between employment and unemployment were the apple sellers on city street corners during the depression. The International Apple Shippers Association had a huge surplus of apples that would not keep for very long. They offered to sell them on credit to jobless people, who would in turn sell them on the streets for a nickel apiece.

By early November 1930 there were 6,000 apple sellers in New York City, and the plan spread to other American cities. (Interestingly, by 1931 certain community groups in Manhattan complained about the mess on the sidewalks from apple cores, so in some parts of the city the apple sellers were forbidden.)

NOT JUST A CITY PROBLEM

The cities were not the only places hard hit during the early 1930s. In fact, the farming communities of America were the first to feel the effects of the depression—even before the stock market collapsed in October 1929. Because farmers were not among the rich or powerful in America, the economic collapse they faced was for the most part ignored by Washington politicians.

The problems began for the farmer immediately after World War I. During the

*A truckload of unem-
ployed men given
temporary jobs as
apple merchants*

*A familiar sight
during the 1930s: A
man sells apples on
a corner.*

war, American farmers were asked to grow record amounts of food, not only for American people but also for our allies in Europe whose land was being used as battlefields.

After the war there was no need for so much food, since European farmers resumed growing their own. But what could be done with all the crops that American farmers were harvesting? With every new crop, the warehouses bulged. And because the supply was so plentiful, the price farmers received for their crops went down.

In an effort to help the farmers, the government suggested that they plant fewer crops. Perhaps the price would rise as the demand went up. But that strategy soon proved to be ineffective, for although farmers cut their production, the price they received continued to plummet. By 1931 corn had dropped to 15 cents a bushel, beef to just over 2 cents a pound. It was costing farmers more to grow and harvest their crops than they received.

In frustration, farmers allowed wheat to rot in the fields. Milk was dumped into ditches or fed to hogs rather than being sold for a loss. And cattle and other livestock were shot, for farmers could not afford to feed them.

A South Dakota woman remembers how horrified she was as a child when her father and other neighbors decided they had no choice but to kill many of their livestock. ''At the far end of our pasture, officials set up a city dump ground, actually a slaughtering area,'' she writes. ''There the bony, old sick cattle would be hauled out in any kind of vehicle, lined up beside the deep trenches to fall therein when shot. I shall forever hear the echo of those shots from inside our house even though we tightly closed the doors and windows. Dad came in late in the day and said, 'They're shooting the bulls now. It will be over soon.'''[11]

''NEITHER BUY NOR SELL AND LET THE TAXES GO TO HELL''

Although farm prices continued to drop, feed, fertilizer, machinery, and taxes continued to increase. So although farmers were growing less, their expenses continued at a higher rate. The result was a lot of farmers who couldn't meet payments and lost their farms.

The reaction of farmers was often uncontrolled anger. ''If they come to take my farm,'' seethed one farmer, ''I'm going to fight. I'd rather be killed outright than die by starvation. But before I die, I'm going to set fire to my crops, I'm going to burn my house! I'm going to [poison] my cattle!''[12]

A mock funeral for the Depression in Boston

Other farmers channeled their anger by forming unions, called Holiday Associations. These farmers tried to withhold their crops from market, hoping to drive prices up to a decent level. They formed barricades on country roads to prevent other farmers from selling their crops and livestock. Their motto was "Neither buy nor sell and let the taxes go to hell."

But no matter how they tried, the farmers were not able to ward off disaster. Prices continued to drop, and more and more farmers were drowning in debt. Between 1930 and 1935 more than 750,000 farms were lost through foreclosure. Farmers with no land to farm moved aimlessly through the country, often in broken-down automobiles pulled by tired plowhorses.

Whether in city breadlines or on backcountry roads, the American people were losing the battle with the economy. What was the answer? And why didn't President Hoover do something?

A man refuses to shave as a symbol of protest against the actions of Herbert Hoover toward veterans.

CHAPTER THREE

TIME FOR A CHANGE

As the Great Depression wore on, most Americans found a target for their anger and frustration—President Herbert Hoover. He was an easy target, too, for his cold, aloof appearance gave him the look of an uncaring, unsympathetic man. He seldom smiled in public, and he wore high starched collars that made him look severe and old-fashioned.

Hoover was a very wealthy man, too—a fact that increased the gap between him and the American standing in a breadline. Working as a civilian engineer, Hoover had become a self-made millionaire—four times over. The president believed that by hard work and perseverance anyone could become rich. "If a man has not made a million by the time he is forty," Hoover once remarked, "then he is not worth much." [1]

And Hoover's advisers and assistants often presented a callous attitude to the public. The secretary of the treasury, Andrew Mellon, actually proclaimed that it might not be a bad thing if the economy hit rock bottom, for it might "weed out" the lazy and shiftless Americans. "People will work harder, live a more moral life," he declared. "Values will be adjusted and enterprising people will pick up the wrecks from less competent people." [2]

Such statements did little to make the American people feel that they had a supporter in the White House. Hoover rapidly became the butt of a great many jokes during the depression. Besides naming the tar paper communities Hoovervilles, the public had a large variety of other uses for the Hoover name. Newspapers that the homeless used to stuff in their clothing for extra warmth were termed "Hoover blankets." Poor people in the rural South hunted jackrabbits, which they called "Hoover hogs." And turned-out, empty pants pockets were known as "Hoover flags."

AN UNFAIR PORTRAYAL

Herbert Hoover was so vilified, in fact, that the depression was known to many people as the "Hoover depression." Author Russell Baker recalls how as a young boy his aunt Pat informed him, "People were starving because of Herbert Hoover. My mother was out of work because of Herbert Hoover. Men were killing themselves because of Herbert Hoover, and their fatherless children were being packed away to orphanages . . . because of Herbert Hoover."[3]

Historians are quick to point out that such accusations were not completely fair. Hoover had been something of a hero during and after World War I, as a matter of fact. He had been the United States food administrator, helping Americans economize so that there was enough to send to troops and allies in Europe. Some historians estimate that Hoover's organized shipments of food and supplies to the war-ravaged European nations saved upward of 100 million lives.

And in contrast to the mockery of his name during the depression, Hoover's name was used in extremely complimentary ways during the years of World War I. To "hooverize" was a common American term, meaning "to economize for a

Herbert Hoover addresses the country over the radio.

good purpose.'' Even in Europe, Hooverstrassen and other variants of his name were used in naming streets and parks to honor Herbert Hoover for his humanitarian contributions.

FIGHTING "THE DOLE"

It was not that Hoover was uncaring about the victims of the depression, say historians. But as the depression deepened and people wanted the government to do something, Hoover dug in his heels and refused.

He was a conservative Republican, and Republicans believe that it is important for government to stay clear of banks, the stock market, and other aspects of business. The fewer government regulations and involvements in the economy, the Republicans say, the stronger the nation's business community will be.

This hands-off approach also applied to people. Hoover believed that people in need should be helped, but not by the federal government. There were churches and private charities that were set up for just those reasons.

"If you let the federal government help the individual," said Hoover, "soon the federal government will control that individual."[4] And that would lead to socialism, an economic system in which the government owns and controls everything. That, said Hoover and his aides, would be exactly the opposite idea of the nonmeddling federal government that the nation's founders had originally intended.

For this reason, Hoover refused to set up any relief programs for families hurt by the depression. He felt that once people were "on the dole," as he called it, they would be less likely to want to work. They would be bound forever to the charity of the government. Better, Hoover insisted, that the burden of such charity be borne by local governments and private organizations like the Salvation Army.

But because times were tight, Americans were not contributing to private charities as they did in more prosperous times. And local governments were floundering in economic hardships, too, which made them ineffective in helping the poor. The result was that less than one-sixth of the people who desperately needed help were getting any.

Finally, after being harshly criticized for doing nothing about the worsening crisis, Hoover established the Reconstruction Finance Corporation. The RFC was like a glorified government credit agency, loaning $2 billion to banks, insurance companies, and railroads to keep them in business.

The hope was that by pumping money into these institutions, it would seep down to the unemployed at the bottom of the economic ladder. In theory the idea seemed plausible, but it proved to be worthless to the people who really needed relief. Critics called it a ''business breadline,'' and chastised Hoover for being more generous with the bankers and financiers of the nation than with the poor. Months after the RFC's formation, it was clear that those people had not received a drop of relief.

By 1932 the frustration and despair felt by so many Americans were surfacing as violence. More and more, the unemployed were banding together, sometimes to demand free food from grocery stores, sometimes to demand jobs to keep from starving.

In one much-publicized incident, 3,000 jobless men in Dearborn, Michigan, stormed the Ford Motor Plant on a freezing morning in March 1932. The men wanted to present a petition at the plant demanding that they be given jobs. However, when they reached the doors of the factory, police tried to turn them back with tear gas. The workers fought back with stones and bits of ice. Finally, police opened fire with their guns, killing four and wounding scores more.

THE BONUS ARMY

But there was no depression protest as infamous as the one staged by a group of World War I veterans in the late spring and summer of 1932. It was known as the Bonus March.

Following the war the U.S. government had voted to extend a cash bonus to all who had fought, as a way of thanking them. The bonus was not to be paid immediately, but rather, it was to come in 1945. Unfortunately, however, many veterans were unemployed in 1932, and could not wait another 13 years for their money. Wouldn't it be possible, they asked, for Congress to grant them their money immediately?

In the spring of 1932 a group of veterans assembled in Portland, Oregon, to organize a nationwide march. The veterans named themselves the Bonus Expeditionary Force, and called for all World War I veterans to meet them in Washington, D.C., in order to take up their plea with Hoover and the Congress.

Thousands showed up in Washington, hoping that their presence there would influence the vote in Congress in a positive way. Some had hitchhiked; other had hopped freight trains. All had been warned by the protest's organizers: ''Stay until the bonus is granted; no radical talk; no panhandling; no booze.''[5]

Participants in the 1932 Bonus March

The first veterans to arrive in Washington during the Bonus March

A Bonus Marcher and his family in the tent they lived in while in Washington, D.C.

By mid-June there were close to 20,000 veterans (many with their families) camped in an area near the Capitol called Anacostia Flats. Most of the veterans had built makeshift dwellings from tar paper and cardboard, giving the place the look of a huge Hooverville.

Yet even though the Bonus Army was large, it was not rowdy or menacing. Historian Frederick Lewis Allen reports that the Washington superintendent of police, General Pelham D. Glassford, saw the Bonus Army as "citizens who had every right to petition the government for a redress of grievances. He helped them to get equipment for their camp and treated them with unfailing consideration."[6]

"OUR GOVERNMENT CANNOT BE COERCED BY MOB RULE"

But to President Hoover and some others in Washington, the presence of the Bonus Army *was* threatening. The veterans were a reminder that the economy had failed even its most honored heroes—as if the nation needed one more reminder about the victims of the depression. President Hoover called the Bonus Army "communists" and "criminals," and warned that the government would not be intimidated by them.

On June 15 the House of Representatives passed the Bonus Bill, but the Senate's approval was also needed. As thousands of veterans gathered on the steps of the Capitol to await the Senate's decision on June 17, the bill was voted down.

Walter Waters, the leader of the Bonus Army, announced the sad news to his "troops." But if people in Washington were waiting for riots to break out, they were mistaken. Instead, the thousands of veterans began softly singing "America." They were disappointed, but not surprised at the outcome. About 5,000 decided to leave Washington; the rest planned to stay on, since they had nowhere else to go.

But Hoover wanted all of them out. He alerted the army chief of staff, Douglas MacArthur, to make sure that the crowds were dispersed. And in a show of unnecessary force, MacArthur and his troops marched on Anacostia Flats, with four troops of cavalry, four companies of infantrymen, machine gunners—even several tanks!

The attack that ensued was shamefully lopsided—the veterans had even cheered as MacArthur's parade approached, for they did not realize its purpose. Within minutes the violence erupted, "cavalrymen were riding into the crowd, infantrymen were throwing tear-gas bombs, women and children were being trampled and were choking from the gas."[7]

Many others were attacked with swords and bayonets. Historian Robert McElvaine writes that "a seven-year-old boy who tried to go back to his tent for his pet rabbit was stabbed in the leg by a soldier who shouted, 'Get out of here, you little son of a bitch!'"[8] In less than a few hours, MacArthur and his troops had burned and destroyed the entire camp of the Bonus Army.

There were four deaths resulting from MacArthur's attack of the Bonus Army at Anacostia Flats, and hundreds of injuries. President Hoover stated after the attack, "A challenge to the authority of the United States government has been met swiftly and firmly. Our government cannot be coerced by mob rule."[9]

But Hoover's assessment of the situation differed drastically from that of many Americans, who felt sympathy for the veterans. With the presidential election less than four months away, that summer of 1932 was a nervous, restless time for the American people. Their faith had diminished, not only in the nation's economy, but in their government. What was happening in America, when heroes of World War I were termed criminals and driven away by force?

As one historian commented, "The person elected president in 1932 would have what might well be the last chance to save the system through peaceful change."[10] And more than ever before, it was becoming clear that that person would not be Herbert Hoover.

Police try to hold back a line of Bonus Marchers as they approach the Capitol.

The Capitol is obscured by smoke as military troops set fire to the Bonus Army camps.

NO CHOICE

The Republican party did nominate Hoover to run again in 1932, however. Although it was certain that as the most hated man in America, he didn't stand a chance against whomever the Democrats would nominate, the Republicans really had no choice but to stick with Hoover.

"President Hoover knew he couldn't win again," writes one historian, "and the convention that picked him knew it, but the party could not dump him without repudiating itself and in effect taking the blame for the depression." [11]

So Hoover was chosen as the Republican standard bearer in 1932. The Democrats, on the other hand, were jubilant. They knew that anyone they nominated would almost be certain to beat Hoover. Their choice was the popular governor of New York, Franklin Delano Roosevelt.

Born in 1882 to a very wealthy New York family, he was a distant cousin of former president Theodore Roosevelt. Franklin Roosevelt had always admired his cousin's accomplishments, and tried very hard to pattern his political career after Theodore's.

He had critics, however. Those who had known Roosevelt at Harvard and Columbia Law School said that he had been far more interested in parties and social events than in studying. Some even joked that the F.D. in his name stood for "Feather Duster"—indicating that intellectually he was something of a lightweight.

But Roosevelt was determined to succeed, and it seemed for a while that his ascent on the political ladder would follow his cousin Teddy's. Having been elected to the New York State Senate in 1910 and appointed assistant secretary of the navy under Woodrow Wilson in 1913, Roosevelt was a rising star. At the rate he was moving, the presidency seemed a likely part of his future.

"TO THE DEPTHS OF TROUBLE"

Roosevelt's career came to an abrupt halt in 1921 when he was struck by a dangerous disease called polio. Polio was greatly feared in those days, for it was highly contagious. There was no serum that could immunize people from polio, and for those who contracted it, it was often fatal.

Roosevelt's bout with the disease left his legs completely paralyzed. And although he had feeling in his arms, the muscles were like jelly. His mother urged him to give up politics and to engage in quieter pursuits, but Roosevelt refused to spend the rest of his life in a wheelchair. He began a vigorous program of therapy to regain the use of his arms. And he would need to learn to walk a new way, with the use of a cane, 14-pound iron leg braces, and the steady, supporting arm of one of his sons.

His goal was difficult, especially in the 1920s. Physically handicapped people were viewed with pity and embarrassment. "If they were not locked up permanently in hospitals," one historian writes, "they were hidden away in their homes. Public schools turned them away, and few hospitals had programs to teach them skills for coping with their disabilities." [12]

Roosevelt spent months in the South, swimming and sitting for hours in warm mineral baths. Although his legs remained shriveled and twisted owing to muscle spasms, the top part of his body grew strong. As he recovered physically, he grew more confident about what he might do with the rest of his life. It was no surprise to

"MY MISSUS"

President Roosevelt's physical handicap made it difficult for him to view firsthand many of the areas hardest hit by the depression. He left a good deal of such traveling to the person he referred to as "my eyes and ears"—his wife, Eleanor Roosevelt. In a crumbling ghetto on Chicago's South Side, in the coal mines of West Virginia, riding a city bus in New York—people were never sure where she would turn up. But in the years of Franklin Roosevelt's presidency, Eleanor became as well known as her husband.

She had lots of energy, and was a good listener. So when she had an opportunity to visit a migrant worker camp or a soup kitchen in a city slum, she did it. She talked with the people, and seemed really to care about what problems they faced and what they thought should be done. These conversations she would carry back to her husband, who frequently quoted her in his meetings with the cabinet.

Eleanor Roosevelt had many critics in America. Politically, she was further to the left than her liberal husband, and for that she was looked upon as a threat to big business and industry. Many thought she had too much influence, that Franklin listened to her perhaps more than he should. But she did not let such criticism interfere with her life. In *The New Deal and War*, William Leuchtenburg quotes her as saying, "I always looked at everything from the point of view of what I *ought* to do, rarely from what I wanted to do."

his family and friends when he decided to reenter political life in 1928, running for the office of governor of New York.

The time he had been away from politics could have put him at a disadvantage, but those who knew him well say that he profited from his bout with polio. Some of his friends felt that his illness caused him to be introspective and to understand what it felt like to be a victim. And since Roosevelt grew up with every possible advantage, such an experience was probably new.

Frances Perkins, a colleague from the New York legislature, claimed that Roosevelt was a changed man after his battle against polio. "The man emerged completely warmhearted with humility of spirit and with a deeper philosophy," she said. "Having been to the depths of trouble, he understood the problems of people in trouble." [13]

THE "LADY IN LABOR"

One of the most influential members of Franklin Roosevelt's administration was Frances Perkins, secretary of labor. She was the first woman ever to serve on a presidential cabinet in the United States, and Roosevelt took great delight in introducing her as "our lady in labor." Throughout the New Deal years she was a familiar public figure in her trademark three-cornered hat.

Perkins began her public service career in New York State, just as Roosevelt did. When he was a state senator in New York, Perkins worked as secretary of the New York Consumers' League. She worked tirelessly, investigating the conditions under which women and children factory employees worked, and lobbying the state legislature for laws that would protect them. (In those days there were no laws prohibiting factory owners from hiring children, or from forcing employees to work 12- to 15-hour days.)

If there was one single occasion that motivated her in her career, Perkins often said, it was the tragic fire at the Triangle Shirtwaist Company in New York City in 1911. In that Saturday afternoon fire, 147 women and girl employees died in the blaze. It was determined after the tragedy that most of the victims could have escaped had employers not kept the workers locked inside during their shift.

Frances Perkins was furious at the injustice of it all, and henceforth became an aggressive advocate for labor reform, especially for child labor laws and safety regulations that would protect workers.

"EVERYTHING ELSE SEEMS EASY"

Roosevelt was elected governor of New York in 1928, and almost immediately set his sights on becoming president. As the Great Depression worsened, and as it became more clear that Hoover was unable to do anything to stop it, Roosevelt knew he had a chance. He began actively campaigning for the Democratic nomination in 1932.

But even though his physical handicap had helped him become more sensitive and caring, there were some who saw it as a liability. Political opponents circulated rumors that the paralysis would become worse, and that he did not have the stamina for being president. There were wilder rumors, too, that the polio had affected Roosevelt's powers of reasoning, and that his brain was damaged.

Roosevelt did not allow such rumors to affect his campaign. If he could beat the disease, he could certainly defeat such underhanded political opponents. "If you have spent two years in bed, trying to wiggle your big toe," he remarked, "everything else seems easy." [14]

His response to the charges about his failing health was intense activity. Although he could easily have relied on radio to carry his speeches to the American people, he wanted to prove that he was strong and capable. So he undertook a grueling 25,000-mile campaign trip meant to put the issue of his health to rest once and for all.

Governor Franklin D. Roosevelt shakes hands with a supporter as his campaign train pulls into Washington, D.C.

He visited nearly every state in the union, and gave hundreds of speeches. Since these were the days before handicapped facilities in buildings, it was often difficult for him to maneuver with his braces and canes. Some of his aides suggested that he use a wheelchair, but Roosevelt felt that the chair made him appear frail, so he refused. He decided it was better to be viewed without help of any kind.

His car was equipped with a sturdy steel bar so that he could pull himself up to a standing position when he wanted to give a speech while keeping his legs hidden from view. Biographer Rebecca Larsen writes that during one such speech, Roosevelt told his audience about his hectic traveling and speaking schedule, and then joked, ''Too bad about this unfortunate sick man, isn't it?'' [15] The audience loved it.

SHARP CONTRASTS

The campaign brought out sharp contrasts between Franklin Roosevelt and President Hoover. Hoover remained aloof and dour, although his campaign managers tried to put forth the image of a kind man who had simply been the victim of circumstances. ''He was described as a brilliant engineer,'' writes one historian, ''whose genius would slowly but surely fix everything if the American voter would only trust him a bit longer.'' [16]

But the voters had had enough. A popular joke of the times was that the ''Great Engineer'' had quickly drained, ditched, and damned the country. And the term Hoover used in describing hardworking Americans—''rugged individualism''— was sarcastically changed to ''ragged individualism'' by his critics.

Roosevelt, on the other hand, was a breath of hope. He seemed to exude confidence. As one writer remembers, ''The grin, the battered old felt hat, the jauntily clenched cigarette holder were a happy contrast to [Roosevelt's] dour opponent. The tragic illness he had endured and surmounted made many feel that, rich though he was, he could understand the suffering and poverty of those who struggled to make a living.'' [17]

Roosevelt's record as governor, too, indicated that he had been responsive to victims of the depression. He had created the nation's first system of unemployment relief in New York, and had begun other programs for public welfare. He had appropriated state funds to relieve New York's hard-hit farmers, and had begun a pension plan to help the elderly.

Roosevelt promised a "New Deal" in his speech to the Democratic convention in Chicago in July 1932. He did not specify what that New Deal would be, and a few political writers found his vagueness troublesome. However, the voters in November were not bothered. The results were not surprising—an overwhelming Roosevelt victory. He carried all but six states, getting 22 million votes to Hoover's 15 million. Whatever it would be, the age of the New Deal had come.

FDR delivers his famous "New Deal" speech

FDR scans the election returns in the newspaper after his easy victory over Hoover.

The Roosevelt family

CHAPTER FOUR

FROM TALK TO ACTION

In the United States there is now a law that says a new president takes office on the January 20 following the election. But in 1932, there was no such law. A new president had to wait until March 4, nearly four months after the election, to take over the office. And in 1932, those four months proved to be the most disastrous in the nation's history.

DETERIORATION OF THE BANKS

Hoover blamed it on people's nervousness about the new president, and his critics blamed it on Hoover's inaction. Whatever the reason, the banking system—shaky since the stock market collapse in 1929—was deteriorating steadily during the winter of 1932–1933.

As people had less faith in the economy, they chose to withdraw their money from banks, rather than risk losing it. As time went by and withdrawals continued to outnumber deposits, most banks suffered from a shortage of money. In some cases, the Federal Reserve and the RFC came to the rescue, pumping millions of dollars into the dying banks.

For a while this worked. Bank customers saw that their neighborhood bank could cover withdrawals and still stay in business, so they relaxed a little. The constant run on the banks seemed to slow. But in the winter of 1932, large numbers of banks began to falter.

In most cases, individual states had no choice but to close down the banks for a certain length of time. People were told that the banks were on a "holiday" and that they would reopen when it was possible. Nevada's banks went on holiday right after the election. Louisiana's closed eight weeks later. And by March, Alabama, California, Idaho, Kentucky, Maryland, Michigan, Mississippi, and Tennessee had all closed down their banks, to the dismay of their customers. There simply wasn't enough cash. Banking is a business that depends on trust and public confidence and there was precious little of either one in 1932–1933.

President Hoover, realizing too late that something had to be done, that the economy was not going to fix itself, tried to reverse the trend. He and his advisers developed plans that he hoped might work. Aware that the public no longer trusted him, Hoover asked Roosevelt to get involved in this last-ditch effort. Would Roosevelt, in a show of unity, publicly support the president's program? It would, Hoover believed, be the only way the program could succeed.

But Roosevelt would not cooperate. He met with the president twice, but reminded Hoover that until March 4, he was a private citizen. He would take no action until he had been sworn in. As one historian comments, ''It was unreasonable to expect [Roosevelt] to tie himself to the policies of an unsympathetic and already discredited administration.'' [1] It was better, Roosevelt felt, to have a clean slate on March 4. Hoover was furious, but there was nothing he could do.

On the morning of Inauguration Day, Hoover was told by his advisers that the governors of two very important states, Illinois and New York, had added their states to the huge list of states whose banks had closed. The nation's banking system, Hoover was informed, had shut down completely. More than 5,000 banks had closed their doors. Those that were still operating were doing so on a limited basis. And to add to the list of failures in Hoover's administration, the president of the New York Stock Exchange, Richard Whitney, announced that morning that, for the first time in its history, the exchange had closed down. With one-fourth of its work force unemployed, its banks locked and dark, its stock exchange abandoned, the United States seemed to be teetering on the edge of complete and utter disaster.

A DREARY INAUGURATION DAY

The weather on March 4, 1933, seemed to match the nation's economic mood. It was cold and gray, with a dismal cold rain that fell intermittently throughout the morning. Even so, there were crowds gathering on the east lawn of the Capitol, where the swearing-in ceremony would take place. And there were people gathering along the route from the White House to the Capitol. It was the custom for the president-elect and the president to ride together from the White House to the ceremony.

Accompanied by their son, James, Franklin and Eleanor Roosevelt arrive at the White House after inauguration ceremonies at the Capitol.

Roosevelt said later that the ride was very uncomfortable. Hoover was still fuming over Roosevelt's refusal to become involved in his financial plans, and he showed it by his cold, stony silence. "He did not so much as glance at his companion [Roosevelt] after his perfunctory handshake," writes historian Kenneth S. Davis, "and he responded not at all to a conversational effort which grew more and more strained on Roosevelt's part." [2]

Davis also reports that Roosevelt later laughingly recalled how he had tried anything to get Hoover to speak to him—at one point even commenting on the "lovely steel" being used in the construction of a government building they passed. At last, Roosevelt gave up and began to enjoy the cheers of the people who lined the streets.

At the Capitol, a huge crowd of more than 100,000 people had gathered in a 40-acre area on the lawn. Hoover stepped unsmilingly to his place on the podium. Roosevelt, locking his leg braces into place and leaning on the arm of his son James, shuffled slowly down the carpeted ramp to the platform.

In addition to the vast crowds watching the ceremony in Washington, D.C., there were millions listening on their radios at home. They were listening carefully for something—perhaps a sign that things might get better. The nation was far worse that day than when Roosevelt had been elected four months earlier. Was there anything he could do to change things?

A CALL TO ACTION

The speech that Roosevelt delivered during the inauguration ceremony is now famous. He knew when he and his advisers wrote the speech that it would set the tone for his presidency. People were depressed and felt hopeless. Some even predicted that Roosevelt, the 32nd president, might be the nation's last president. If the economy did not turn around, many thought, a violent revolution might occur.

Roosevelt's speech was very serious, and he delivered it in a strong, clear, confident voice. He said, "Let me assert my firm belief that the only thing we have to fear is fear itself—nameless, unreasoning, unjustified terror which paralyzes needed efforts to convert retreat into advance." He promised that the United States was not dead, but rather that "this great nation will endure as it has endured, will revive and will prosper." [3]

Roosevelt talked about putting people back to work and making the nation's economy strong again. He did not sound like President Hoover, who had avoided action, thinking the economy would heal itself. Roosevelt made no hollow promises of prosperity being "just around the corner"—a phrase the American people had heard too many times to believe.

Instead, Roosevelt seemed like a man who was ready to take action—immediately. He spoke about asking Congress "for the one remaining instrument to meet the crisis—broad Executive power to wage a war against the emergency." [4] This made sense to many Americans listening that day. Here was a president who admitted that there was a national emergency. And Roosevelt talked like a man ready to assume control and do battle with the problems of the nation's faltering economy. He seemed ready for action.

ACTING FAST

The American public did not have to wait long for Roosevelt to act. The very next day, Sunday, March 5, he called on Congress to meet in a special session, beginning that very Thursday. There was a great deal of work to be done, and Congress was needed to do it.

He also announced that beginning the following day, all of the nation's banks would be closed during the next week for a bank holiday. At the end of a week, some banks would reopen, but only those that the government had found to be strong and sound. In addition, Roosevelt announced that he was halting the export of gold out of the country.

The issue of gold was a serious one. In those days, American currency was backed by gold, as was the currency of France, Germany, and other of America's important European trading partners. An ounce of gold was worth a certain number of French francs, German marks, or American dollars. Because of the gold standard, these nations could do business and be confident that they were paying the correct price. All of the gold backing America's currency was kept at Fort Knox, Kentucky.

But with rising panic over the economy, few people had any confidence in American dollars. Instead, more and more people demanded payment in gold. This was especially true of foreign investors, who had been pulling out of American markets, taking large amounts of gold with them. The gold supply in America was being depleted, and unless something was done soon, the currency used in the United States would be worthless.

So between the bank holiday and the halt on gold exports, the economy of the

United States was temporarily on hold. During this period, Roosevelt would have time to regroup, looking carefully at the options he had to make changes. And while the president and his advisers were looking at their choices, the American people wondered how they were going to live for the next several days in a world without money!

JIGSAW PUZZLES, TOOTHPASTE,
AND OTHER CURRENCY

Some politicians worried when Roosevelt made his announcement. They feared that riots would ensue, with people panicking and fearful. Surprisingly, however, the mood of the country was a mixture of excitement and relief. At last the problem was out in the open, and it was being dealt with. Few people had any reserves of cash, but everyone seemed to be in the same boat.

Frederick Lewis Allen writes that the shops and businesses were all but deserted, for no one had money to spend. "There was a Saturday air about the business offices, trains were sparsely filled. . . . But in the talk that buzzed everywhere there was less of foreboding than of eager and friendly excitement. . . . 'You say you had thirty dollars on you when the banks closed? Well, you're in luck. I had only three-fifty—I'd planned to go to the bank that morning.'" [5]

Everyone, it seems, has stories to tell about that week without money. How did people manage? Sometimes businesses issued *scrip,* a kind of money that could be redeemed for the real thing when the banks finally opened. In other cases, people used their imaginations and bartered rather than bought. An Oklahoma hotel, for instance, offered to take food items for their coffee shop in exchange for a room for the night. The offer worked out, for the coffee shop received eggs, vegetables, chickens, and even a pig!

The people at Madison Square Garden offered to take everything from toothpaste to jigsaw puzzles to spark plugs in exchange for tickets for the week's boxing match. And one newspaper in Iowa even offered a barter deal for prospective customers. The newspaper would give you a year's subscription for 10 bushels of wheat—two years' for 18 bushels.

In other places, people used stamps, foreign currency, and personal IOUs. Oddly enough, those who had been lucky enough to have a supply of cash on hand didn't always have an easy time. Someone needing a nickel for a pay telephone or change for cigarettes often searched in vain for change for a $20 bill.

FOLKSY, NOT FORMAL

It was after his first week in office, on Sunday evening, March 12, that Roosevelt decided to touch base with the American people in a radio broadcast. The purpose, he said, was to reassure them, and explain the actions that he had taken that week.

The idea was eagerly embraced by radio networks. The president was given a choice of two kinds of introductions by the announcers—formal or folksy. Roosevelt went with folksy. And so, just before the president came on the air, the silky-voiced announcer greeted the estimated 60 million listeners with the words, "The president wants to come into your home and sit at your fireside for a little fireside chat."[6] Although it may seem contrived by modern standards, the idea was a smashing success. The "fireside chats," as they were henceforth known, were to become a tradition of the Roosevelt administration.

Roosevelt began each one with the words, "My friends." He spoke in clear, simple language to explain the things he had done. In that first "chat," he told the

President Roosevelt during a radio broadcast urging voters to elect New Deal candidates to public office.

American people that the banks would begin opening the very next day. He reminded his listeners that if their bank was not open the following day, that did not mean it would stay closed. Only when the federal government could guarantee its safety would each bank reopen.

"I can assure you," Roosevelt told his radio audience, "it is safer to keep your money in a reopened bank than under the mattress."[7]

Roosevelt appealed to the good sense of each of his listeners. He reminded them that it would take courage and confidence to make his plan succeed, but that he believed the American people could rise to the occasion. "You people must have faith; you must not be stampeded by rumors or guesses. Let us unite in banishing fear. We have provided the machinery to restore our financial system; it is up to you to support and make it work. It is your problem no less than it is mine. Together, we cannot fail."[8]

FROM BANKS TO BEER

Even though Roosevelt was convincing, many financial experts were nervous. They worried that with the extended bank holiday, people might be panicky, and make frantic runs on the open banks.

But Roosevelt's words had worked magic. As he had promised, the majority of the American banks reopened the next day. And rather than panicking, people were calm. In fact, deposits outnumbered withdrawals that day by a large margin. In New York City alone, $10 million more was deposited in the city's banks than withdrawn. By the end of the week the New York Stock Exchange reopened, and stock prices skyrocketed an unbelievable 15 percent. The faith and courage that Roosevelt had asked for in the American people seemed to be paying off.

But there was another issue that the new president wanted resolved during his first days in office. In fact, in the middle of a discussion of the banking crisis with some of his advisers, Roosevelt had leaned back in his chair. "I think," he announced, "now would be a good time for beer."[9]

Roosevelt was referring to an end to Prohibition, the time when the United States had made the drinking, manufacture, and selling of alcoholic beverages illegal. Although there were still some who felt alcohol was an evil that needed to be banned, most Americans were for the repeal of the Prohibition laws.

During the first days of his administration, Roosevelt felt the nation needed a break from Prohibition. He hurried through a modification of a bill that was already before Congress to allow the sale and consumption of low-alcohol beer and wine.

"He gave us back the banks and beer in one week," remembers Miles Van Horner, a Wisconsin hardware dealer during the depression. "What more could the country ask? If the fellow didn't do another deed his whole time in the White House, I guess we'd have been happy for that much!"[10]

THE BRAIN TRUST

But there was more to be done if the nation's economy was to become strong and stable once again. The banking crisis had been averted, and beer had been legalized, but nothing more. A full quarter of the nation's work force was unemployed, and six million people were on the charity rolls across the country. It was necessary to put into play the "New Deal" that the American people had been promised.

Congress had already been called into a special session, so Roosevelt took advantage of the situation. In an unprecedented move, Roosevelt proposed, and the Congress approved, no fewer than 15 new legislative bills aimed at getting the nation back to work and the economy strong again. This time of frenzied activity in Congress and the White House is often referred to as the "Hundred Days."

Roosevelt was not the only motivating force behind all the legislation. He had carefully chosen a number of advisers who he thought would bring a fresh new spirit to his administration. Many of them were professors, young lawyers, and social workers. Very few were politicians.

Dubbed the "Brain Trust" by the press, they were "far younger and much more liberal than those who had surrounded Hoover. Some had even been socialists. Some had been interested in communism. They brought new ideas and a sense of excitement that the capital had not seen in some time."[11]

"PEOPLE DON'T EAT IN THE LONG RUN!"

The first priority of Roosevelt and his Brain Trust was federal relief, a concept that Hoover had scorned for so long. But there were people without food, shelter, or adequate clothing, and they had to be attended to. One of the first proposals Roosevelt pushed through Congress was the Federal Emergency Relief Administration, or FERA. FERA was granted $500 million in aid, which would go from the federal government to each state government.

How the money would be distributed to the individual states was the responsibility of one of Roosevelt's key advisers, a 42-year-old social worker from New

York named Harry Hopkins. Hopkins was known as "the assistant president" because of the amount of work he did. Throughout the depression, Hopkins was the central administrator for all relief efforts.

Raymond Moley, another of the Brain Trust, once said that Hopkins had "a capacity for quick, and, it should be added expensive, activity." [12] Hopkins's first day on the job was proof of that. Both he and Roosevelt believed that immediate distribution of FERA money was important, although Hopkins's office was not yet set up for him. The lack of office space didn't slow him down, however. In his first two hours on the job, Hopkins spent $5 million, working out of packing crates and cardboard boxes in a White House hallway!

The administrator of FERA was sympathetic to the plight of the nation's poor, and more than once he had to remind his colleagues that basic needs had to come before politics. In trying to convince Hopkins of the merits of a certain program, someone told him that the plan "would work in the long run." Hopkins snapped back, "People don't eat in the long run, they eat every day." [13]

It soon became clear to Roosevelt that FERA was only a desperation measure. A strong economy could not be based merely on feeding the hungry. Jobs must be found for the nation's unemployed so that the cycle of poverty could be broken. And the jobs must be real work—jobs that would keep the economy moving, not just "leaf raking" jobs that were no real benefit to anyone.

THE CIVILIAN CONSERVATION CORPS

In late March, Congress approved Roosevelt's plan for the Civilian Conservation Corps, or CCC. The president had always liked the idea of getting people away from the cities, back to the forests and countryside. The CCC was based on just this idea. About 250,000 young men between the ages of 18 and 25 were hired by the government to do construction and conservation work.

The young men were all from poor families, and because they were from urban slums, most had never even seen a forest. This idea appealed to Roosevelt, who had been an ardent outdoorsman and felt that the farther people were from the cities, the better. The young men were housed in military bases throughout the Great Plains and western United States.

They worked hard, from morning until night. They received free room and board, and were paid $30 each month. Of that, they could keep $5; the rest was sent to their families.

Young recruits of the Civilian Conservation Corps get their first taste of army food.

Some were critical of Roosevelt's CCC. They worried it was too militaristic, that in their spruce-green uniforms and military barracks the young men were more like army recruits than civilians. And the fact that the army was directing the bases and training made such critics even more uncomfortable. They pointed to Germany, a dictatorship where unemployed youth were frequently steered into the army. Would that happen in the United States, too?

But the majority of Americans were pleased with the CCC. They were impressed with the large amount of work the young men accomplished—from building dams, roads, and bridges to planting 17 million acres of new forest. The CCC restored historic landmarks and built campgrounds and beaches.

As for the criticism of its being militaristic, Roosevelt called such thinking "utter rubbish." The army was used in organizing, supplying, and transporting the CCC because they were good at it. There were no marches, no drills. And after 6 or 12 months, each young man returned home with better work habits and skills than he had had before, and more self-confident about his future in the job market.

HELPING THE FARMERS

The farmers needed immediate attention from Roosevelt and his Brain Trust, too. The prices that farmers received for their products were lower each season, yet the expenses and taxes farmers paid out continued to rise. To tackle the farm problem, Roosevelt came up with the Agricultural Adjustment Act, or AAA.

The problem, it seemed, was the huge surpluses of grain and other farm commodities. By growing so much, the farmers were driving their prices down. It seemed clear that the days of growing as much as possible, without thinking about

---

BLACK BLIZZARDS

Besides the hard luck with low market prices for their products, farmers on the Great Plains had another nightmare during the 1930s—this one concocted in part by Mother Nature. Drought struck, scorching the earth and turning whatever grew brown. Crops withered and died, and the livestock that depended on the tiny streams and creeks died as well.

But the problem did not stop there. For years, the farmers in the Great Plains regions had been turning over more acres of land, scrambling to increase the growing space in the years of World War I. Because of this, they were known as "sodbusters." In addition, they had overgrazed the land, allowing their cattle and sheep to eat all of the prairie grass whose roots anchored the precious topsoil in place.

With the coming of the drought, there were also high winds and dust storms that literally blew away tens of thousands of acres of farmland. The skies were so black that cars had to drive with their lights on, even during the day. With the valuable topsoil gone, farmers were forced to abandon their acreage. Many of these headed west to California, a place they had been told was brimming with possibilities. Close to 40,000 farmers a year packed up their belongings and left their wind-battered farmsteads behind.

what the market could support, were over. Control was the answer, and the AAA was the agency to help.

Control, simply put, was to limit the number of acres a farmer planted or the number of animals he raised. For instance, as so many farmers were growing record amounts of cotton, the price the farmer received per pound was only four cents—compared with the ten cents it cost to grow the cotton. If farmers could be persuaded to grow less, the price would go up.

That persuasion was done by AAA agents who walked the back roads of rural America, talking to farmers. The agents offered farmers payment for *not* growing crops—a new one on most farmers. In 1933, when the AAA was just getting started, however, the huge new cotton crop had already been planted. The AAA agents were granted $200 million to distribute to farmers who would go into their fields and plow the young plants under.

BURNING ORANGES AND SLAUGHTERED PIGLETS

Corn was another crop that had to be reduced. But besides growing less of it, it was also necessary to reduce the number of corn-eating animals—namely pigs. In a much publicized move in 1933, the AAA ordered and supervised the slaughter of six million baby pigs.

Fruit growers, too, were forced to stand by and watch the oranges they had carefully nurtured be picked and burned in large fires. To many Americans, the killing of the baby pigs and the waste of millions of oranges seemed wrong. Many farmers admitted that the whole idea went against their basic instincts. "It's like a doctor finding ways to hurt people, or something like that," complained one Minnesota farmer.[14]

In his book *The Grapes of Wrath,* John Steinbeck described the sad feelings of farmers who watched as their orange crops went up in flames. "The work of the roots, of the vines, of the trees must be destroyed to keep up the price, and this is the saddest, bitterest thing of all. A million people hungry, needing the fruit, and kerosene sprayed on the golden mountains and the smell of rot fills the country."[15]

Roosevelt's secretary of agriculture, Henry Wallace, didn't like the reduction measures any better than anyone else. But these were desperate times, said Wallace, which called for desperate measures. "We must play with the cards that are dealt," he said. "Agriculture cannot survive in a capitalistic society as a philanthropic [charitable] enterprise."[16]

Knowing that the pigs were used both to make fertilizer and to feed people on relief programs helped a little. So did seeing the rise in prices farmers received for their crops in the following years. Wheat, for instance, had sold for only 38 cents a bushel in 1932, but by 1936 farmers were receiving $1.02. It was difficult to argue with such numbers. For the first time since World War I, American farmers were making a living wage!

THE NATIONAL RECOVERY ADMINISTRATION

One of the most famous of Roosevelt's New Deal agencies was the National Recovery Administration, or NRA. Roosevelt, who was very proud of it, called the congressional act that established the NRA ''the most important and far-reaching legislation ever enacted by the American Congress.''[17]

While the AAA established controls for farmers, the NRA did the same for each industry in the United States. The goal was to stimulate the recovery of the nation's

---

THE WORKS PROGRESS ADMINISTRATION

One of the New Deal agencies that received a great deal of public attention was the Works Progress Administration (WPA). Begun later in the New Deal, the WPA's goal was to replace simple relief programs with work relief. There was no great advantage, Roosevelt believed, in repeatedly giving money to someone. Giving someone charity month after month took away pride. It would be better to create jobs instead.

Congress appropriated $5 billion at first in 1935, then $10 billion more over the next four years. In its time, the WPA put four million unemployed Americans to work, constructing airports, building rural roads that went from farms to markets, and building new schools. In addition, unemployed teachers were paid to teach in big-city ghettos as well as to staff libraries.

One facet of the WPA took out-of-work artists, writers, and musicians and paid them to be creative. Books were written, murals were painted on city walls, and civic and community orchestras were started. Plays that had been seen only by big-city audiences before the depression were taken to the small towns and farming villages in the Midwest. Historians estimate that in four years, some 30 million people in these Midwest communities saw WPA productions!

Workmen put a new coat of paint on a theater marquee as part of the Works Progress Administration program.

factories and industries, and thereby put people back to work. The NRA was unusual in that for the first time, the government was directly involved in the business community.

Under the NRA legislation, businesses were allowed to fix prices that they considered fair for their products. Such price-fixing would eliminate one company from trying to undercut prices to drive another out of business, thereby hurting the whole industry. Therefore, if the price of a ton of steel was set at $300, no steel company was permitted to outsell the others by lowering their price to $250 per ton. Besides setting codes for fair prices, each industry was also encouraged to establish limits for the amount each would produce.

But it was not only the heads of business and industry that were helped by the NRA. The new laws also protected workers by establishing a minimum wage, rules against children working, and a maximum number of hours employers could ask employees to work.

"IRONPANTS" AND THE BIG BLUE BIRD

Roosevelt and his Brain Trust hoped that by following the NRA's proposals, businesses would see higher profits, which would lead to more employment and more money in circulation. If the scheme was to work, however, businesses had to go along with it. Those who voluntarily complied with NRA codes were given a sign to display in their store windows. The sign said We Do Our Part, and had a picture of a big blue eagle clutching a cogwheel in its talons.

The job of persuading business to "go NRA" fell to one of Roosevelt's most colorful aides, Hugh Johnson. Johnson was a tough, leather-faced ex-cavalry officer from World War I. Because of his ability during the war to ride his horse for hours without getting sore, he was nicknamed "Ironpants" by his fellow officers. The name stuck long after the war was over.

Using every ounce of salesmanship he possessed (which was quite a bit!), Johnson traveled the country, pleading, begging, threatening—whatever it took to drum up support for the NRA. According to historians, Johnson ran the NRA like a war campaign—and he was the general and head drill sergeant all rolled into one.

He told the American women that they were important soldiers in the battle against the depression. "It is zero hour for housewives," he thundered. "Their battle cry is 'Buy now under the Blue Eagle!'" [18]

To raise enthusiasm and public support, the NRA sponsored gala events with movie stars, singers, and comedians. There were colorful parades with floats decorated with huge blue eagles. And, remembers historian Robert Bendiner, "over all the national excitement could be heard the raucous voice of the barrel-chested trainer of the Blue Eagle, 'Ironpants' Johnson, threatening to 'crack down on the chiselers,' promising to give code resisters 'a sock right on the jaw,' and invoking God's mercy on those who attempted to 'trifle with this bird.' " [19]

THE END OF THE HONEYMOON?

The Hundred Days was a flurry of activity for the president and the Congress. Such unity of purpose between the White House and Congress is usually rare, and not since Roosevelt's first administration has so much been accomplished so quickly. And the results seemed promising. After the first year and a half of the New Deal, five million of America's unemployed had found work.

But the CCC, the AAA, the NRA, and the dozen more agencies that made up the alphabet soup of the New Deal were not without their critics. Of course, everyone knew that the "honeymoon"—that time when the nation was so enraptured with their new president that in their eyes he could do no wrong—could not last forever. By the end of 1934, there were other voices besides those praising President Roosevelt. And those voices seemed to be getting louder.

Eleanor Roosevelt serves soup at a food kitchen.

CHAPTER FIVE

VOICES OF DISCONTENT

Franklin Roosevelt might have been hailed as a superman in 1932 as he took office, but by the end of his first year as president, reality had set in. The New Deal programs had put millions back to work, but there were still millions more without work. There had been months of improvement with definite signs of recovery, but there also had been months in which the economy slipped downward.

"The economic system had pulled out of its sinking spell of 1929–33," reports one historian, "only to become a chronic invalid, whose temperature was lower now in the mornings, but showed no signs of returning quickly to normal. Americans were getting used to the fact that nine or ten million of their fellow countrymen were out of work." [1]

And because recovery had not been automatic, Roosevelt began to be the focus of criticism by various groups of Americans.

COMPLAINTS FROM THE RICH

Some of Roosevelt's most harsh criticism came from the powerful people—the owners of businesses and captains of industry, bankers, investors, and other wealthy people. These people, whose banks, businesses, and investments were being threatened, were very relieved when Roosevelt took office. Yet, as historians have noted wryly, as soon as they were saved, the nation's rich began to get nervous. As Roosevelt and his Brain Trust put more and more New Deal programs into practice, the wealthy discovered that Roosevelt's goal was not to get things back to the way they were before the stock market crash of 1929, but rather to change and reform the nation's economy.

"He set out to champion the less fortunate, to denounce such financiers and big

Out-of-work men are fitted for clothes and shoes as part of a government-sponsored relief program.

A young woman sits down to a meal at a 1¢ cafeteria in Boston.

business men as stood in his way," says historian Frederick Lewis Allen, "and as their opposition to him hardened, so also did his opposition to them."[2]

The biggest complaints from the well-to-do concerned one of the New Deal's most talked-about programs, the NRA. They felt that far too much had been granted labor by the new program. With workers able to organize unions, to strike against their employers, and to collectively bargain, it seemed to the wealthy as though the workers had been given too much control.

When Roosevelt pushed new taxes on the rich through Congress for the purpose of funding more New Deal legislation, that was the last straw. His political enemies branded him a socialist, saying that if Roosevelt had his way, the federal government would be running everything, and that private enterprise would be a thing of the past. Rumors abounded that Roosevelt and his Brain Trust wanted to "Russianize" America, and make the nation a dictatorship.

THE NEW BONUS ARMY

In the late spring of 1933, after Roosevelt had been president for several weeks, a new Bonus Expeditionary Force began trickling into Washington, D.C. The first Bonus Army had, of course, been violently routed out of its shabby campsites the previous summer by some of President Hoover's most trusted army officers.

But some of the veterans returned, hoping that a new president would somehow mean new hope for their cause, which was early payment of a bonus promised to them at the end of World War I. The answer, unfortunately, was the same, although the terms were pleasantly different from those of Hoover.

For one thing, Roosevelt had real sympathy for the men's cause. He assigned his most trusted aide, Louis Howe, to make sure the veterans had three hot meals each day. And instead of camping out, the veterans were allowed to stay in an old army barracks near the Capitol. Besides that, the Bonus Army, whose numbers had swelled to 3,000 within a few weeks, was visited by Eleanor Roosevelt, who talked with the members at length about their experiences fighting in Europe.

Although Roosevelt was not able to hasten their bonus payments from Congress, he *was* able to get many of them jobs through the Civilian Conservation Corps. The Corps was actually for younger men, but Roosevelt saw to it that age limits were waived. More than 2,600 of the veterans took him up on the idea!

Senator Thomas Schall of Minnesota called the president "Frankenstein Roosevelt" and the NRA blue eagle "that Soviet duck." And Henry Ford, one of the richest, most influential men in America, made no secret of the fact that he refused to support the NRA codes. "Hell, that Roosevelt buzzard!" he scoffed. "I wouldn't put it on the car."[3]

The growing fury among the rich was much publicized for the simple reason that the largest newspapers were run by wealthy families. William Randolph Hearst, one of the most successful newspaper giants in the United States, wrote scathing editorials against Roosevelt and the NRA. Hearst and other newspaper publishers were especially angry about the NRA's banning of child labor, for in those days newspapers depended for their circulation on the young newsboys who worked for ridiculously low wages.

So as Congress and the president continued to grind out new programs, the rich became more angry. Roosevelt was frequently called "a traitor to his class," for he himself had come from a wealthy family. Many refused to refer to him by name, using instead "that lunatic," or, cruelly, "that cripple in the White House." Jokes about a possible presidential assassination were popular, such as: "Did you hear the good news? Roosevelt got shot and Hopkins got killed on the way to the funeral."

Historian Robert Bendiner remembers high-society balls where guests were asked to come dressed as someone they despised. "The invitations specified that no one was to come as the President or his wife," he writes, "for fear that the ballroom would be monotonously jammed with imitation Roosevelts."[4]

CRITICISM FROM THE LEFT

Interestingly, as big business was growing more vocal about what they called Roosevelt's swing toward socialism, prominent American socialists were angry with the president for being too nice to big business. On a political continuum, with the left being socialism, socialists thought Roosevelt too far right. Norman Thomas, a socialist who rejected the New Deal because it was too capitalistic, insisted that the president "did not carry out the Socialist platform unless he carried it out on a stretcher."[5]

Others agreed with Thomas, and the mid-1930s saw several movements from the political left which, at least temporarily, seemed to offer depression-weary Americans a glimmer of hope. One of these was a program called End Poverty in California (EPIC), founded by Upton Sinclair.

Sinclair's name was well known to many Americans, for he had written a popular book in 1906 called *The Jungle*. The book was a graphic look at the meatpacking industry in the United States. The unsanitary conditions described by Sinclair sickened readers, and their disgust resulted in the passage of laws to control the production of food and drugs in the United States.

But in the 1930s Sinclair's cause was poverty. He devised a plan that he claimed would totally eliminate poverty within four years. The plan was socialistic, in that it called for government ownership of all factories and businesses. Large community farms would replace the small family farms in the United States. And because such a large segment of California's population was elderly, Sinclair's plan also called for a monthly pension of $60 to all people over 60.

Upton Sinclair discusses his plans to revitalize California.

DIRTY POLITICS

Upton Sinclair, the Democratic candidate for governor in California, was soundly defeated in 1934. However, most historians feel that it was not Sinclair or his End Poverty in California (EPIC) plan that voters rejected. Quite the contrary—many felt that Sinclair would have been elected had not the opposition waged the dirtiest campaign in the history of state politics.

Two months before the election, many political analysts felt that Sinclair's victory was in the bag—many of his friends in the Democratic party were even calling him "Governor." The Republicans were worried, and they responded by using every kind of political dirty trick that they could come up with.

As historian Robert S. McElvaine writes in *The Great Depression,* lines from Sinclair's novels were taken out of context and ascribed to him personally. The Republicans circulated rumors that he believed in communism, that he was an atheist, and that he was sexually promiscuous, although such statements were completely untrue.

The wealthy Hollywood movie executives were nervous about Sinclair becoming governor, and they created the biggest campaign frauds of all. In addition to threatening to move to another state if Sinclair became governor, they made a series of damaging newsreels. Some showed people with Russian accents (really actors) endorsing Sinclair, while others had weeping women (actors again) crying about what would happen to their savings if Sinclair were elected.

He wrote a book outlining EPIC and his plans for California once he became governor of the state. Entitled *I, Governor of California, and How I Ended Poverty: A True Story of the Future,* the book sold millions of copies. Voters were enthusiastic, and political analysts of the time predicted that Sinclair had a good chance of winning the election. In the end, however, a dirty campaign waged by his opponent ended his political hopes.

TOWNSEND CLUBS

Dr. Francis Townsend was another California Roosevelt critic whose special cause was the elderly. He had become active in this cause after an incident that happened in 1933, shortly after Roosevelt took office. "Looking out the bathroom window while shaving . . . he had been genuinely horrified at the sight of three old women rummaging in a garbage can for scraps of food, and out of his righteous wrath grew the Old Age Revolving Pension plan."[6]

Townsend's plan was that the government pay $200 per month to every American over age 60, provided that each recipient agreed to spend the money within 30 days. Townsend believed that his plan would end the depression, for there would be more money in circulation, in the hands of wise older Americans who would not spend money foolishly.

Many people (most of them elderly) were organized into clubs to support Townsend's political career. At one time in 1936 therewere more than 3.5 million members of 7,000 Townsend Clubs nationwide. However, it was his lack of a workable method for financing his plan that was his downfall as a politician. His idea was to levy a 2 percent income tax to pay for the pensions. Most Americans objected to this, because his tax would be hurting a group that needed help, too— the already-suffering middle class.

THE RADIO PRIEST

One of the most popular of the anti-Roosevelt political extreme was a Catholic priest, Father Charles Edward Coughlin. Father Coughlin had a weekly radio show called "The Golden Hour of the Little Flower," which he broadcast from a suburb of Detroit, Michigan.

Politically, Coughlin began as a Roosevelt supporter in the election of 1932. He called then-president Hoover "the bankers' friend, the Holy Ghost of the rich, the protective angel of Wall Street."[7] He liked Roosevelt, and during the Hundred Days stated frequently in his broadcasts that "the New Deal is Christ's deal."[8]

But he lost patience with Roosevelt and his Brain Trust, believing that the Democratic party was not moving fast enough to solve the problems of poverty. Like Sinclair, Coughlin embraced socialism, claiming that the nation would be better off if the government ran the industries.

Father Coughlin told his listeners that bankers were "devils" and that their overwhelming lust for profits was the cause of the unemployment and widespread poverty in the United States. As for Coughlin himself, he claimed that his task was to remind the government of its moral obligation to the people. "I glory in the fact that I am a simple Catholic priest,'' Coughlin remarked, ''endeavoring to inject Christianity into the fabric of an economic system woven upon the loom of the greedy.''[9]

An anti-Semitic, Coughlin believed that Roosevelt's New Deal had been infested with the wealthy Jewish bankers, and that what had begun as good programs were now corrupt. He called Roosevelt's administration ''government of the bankers, by the bankers, and for the bankers.''

There were apparently many Americans who agreed with Coughlin's ideas. At first a local radio show, ''The Golden Hour of the Little Flower'' grew in popularity in the mid-1930s. CBS picked up the show, broadcasting it over 16 stations nationwide. His shows were the most widely heard radio shows in history, with audiences of 40 million—even more than popular programs like ''Amos 'n Andy'' and ''The Burns and Allen Show.''

However, Coughlin's ideas became more and more radical in the 1930s. He lost most of his popularity as he began to preach about the need for a dictatorship in America, especially when he embraced the political ideals of Adolf Hitler and Benito Mussolini.

Father Coughlin addresses an audience in Cleveland's Public Hall on the subject of peace.

"EVERY MAN A KING"

But it was Senator Huey Long from Louisiana who was the most famous critic of Roosevelt. Long was known to his millions of supporters as "the Kingfish" because of his philosophy of "Every man a king, every girl a queen" that made him so popular in his home state.

Long thought it was disgraceful that there could be multimillionaires in the United States when millions were living below the poverty level. He proposed that the enormous wealth in the United States be shared so that everyone could have enough. He called his program Share Our Wealth.

Under Long's plan, inheritances would be limited to $5 million, and no personal fortune could exceed $8 million. The government's job would be to take control of any excess money and redistribute it among needy families. The goal was to provide every family in America with a free car, a home, a radio, and an annual income of $2,000. In addition, Share Our Wealth would guarantee every young man and woman a free college education.

Most economists of the day rolled their eyes at Share Our Wealth, protesting that such a plan was utterly impossible. Even so, many Americans believed that Long could do it. First as governor and then as senator from Louisiana, he had accomplished miracles. He built roads and improved medical care and education, providing free schoolbooks for all. The underprivileged of Louisiana thought of Huey Long as a saint.

Huey Long had accomplished so much in Louisiana that many Americans were convinced that he could do the same for the country. He ruled his state "with an iron hand," writes one historian, "smashing opposition as ruthlessly as a racketeer." [10] Indeed, most historians agree that Long was a dictator—a kind one to the poor, perhaps, but a dictator nonetheless.

The threat Long posed to Roosevelt's chances of election in 1936 were very real. Long's speeches were full of references to "the forgotten man," a phrase Roosevelt himself had used in the 1932 campaign. Roosevelt had felt that the poor and middle classes were forgotten by government and big business, and his New Deal was aimed at them.

But in 1935 it was Long who was targeting the "forgotten man." He reminded people how they were still suffering the effects of the depression, and told them that Roosevelt's programs weren't any more useful "than a jar of warm spit." [11]

Senator Huey Long gives a speech on the radio.

And many Americans, whose lives hadn't improved substantially since the New Deal began, felt that Long was the man to help them.

Historians say that Long's plan was to run for president—not in 1936 but in 1940. His goal was to campaign against Roosevelt, however, by supporting an independent who would split the Democratic vote. According to Long's plan, Roosevelt would lose to the Republican, who would be so terrible as president that Long himself could step in as the Democratic nominee in 1940 and win. None of this occurred, however, because in September 1935 a Louisiana physician who had a longtime grievance against Long assassinated him.

REVOLUTIONARY LEGISLATION

Partly because of the outcry from the political left about "the forgotten man," Roosevelt signed into law a much-debated piece of the New Deal in the summer of 1935. It was known as the Social Security Act, and the programs it began are just as important today as they were then. The act entitled Americans over age 65 to receive a monthly pension from the federal government. In addition, the Social Security Act provided unemployment insurance and allowed federal aid for the care of children.

It was a revolutionary piece of legislation. Never before in the history of the United States had there been a law dealing with social welfare. Always before, old people had had to depend on private charity when they had financial trouble. For many Americans, the idea of government-sponsored "charity" was hard to swallow, for self-reliance had been a part of American thinking since the nation's beginnings. "Since pioneer days, Americans had taken a fierce pride in their ability to stand on their own feet and not ask for financial assistance from their government," writes one historian.[12]

Because the Social Security Act was such a new concept, there was a great deal of heated controversy over who should and should not be helped by it. Many southerners, for example, worried that guaranteed assistance for the unemployed would result in laziness, especially among African Americans. In a 1935 edition of a Mississippi newspaper, the *Jackson Daily News,* an editorial warns, "The average Mississippian can't imagine himself chipping in to pay pensions for able-bodied Negroes to sit around in idleness . . . while cotton and corn crops are crying for workers to get them out of the grass."[13]

Even with the criticism the bill received from some segments of society, Roosevelt and his Brain Trust were pleased with the Social Security Act. Politically it had been a strong move, for it diluted some of the harshest criticism from the political left. With the passage of the law, Roosevelt demonstrated that he had not forgotten the "forgotten man."

THE LANDSLIDE

Political analysts predicted a close presidential race in 1936. So many newspapers were owned either by conservative Republicans or by Democrats who were frightened by the president's programs that Roosevelt's Republican opponent, Kansas governor Alf Landon, received far more extensive press coverage.

But the analysts and experts were wrong. When the votes were tallied in November, only two states, Maine and Vermont, went to Landon. Roosevelt won by a landslide.

Modern historians offer several explanations. One is simply that Landon's quiet demeanor was a poor match for Roosevelt's energetic campaign style. The president knew better than most in 1936 the value of a good radio voice, and his was superb. Landon often came across limp and lifeless. Besides, say some historians, Landon's speeches were often filled with confusing statements, especially when he spoke off the cuff. "Wherever I have gone in this country," one of his most famous comments went, "I have found Americans." [14] His speeches were so boring, in fact, that one newspaper writer quipped after the election, "If Landon had given one more speech, Roosevelt would have carried Canada, too." [15]

But the most obvious explanation for Roosevelt's one-sided win is that in 1936 most Americans trusted him. While they knew that the depression was not over, and that Roosevelt had not ended unemployment and poverty, people realized that they were better off than they had been four years earlier.

In many cases, President Roosevelt was viewed as a hero, even though he had not achieved everything he had set out to do. "I'd give my heart to the president," wrote one North Carolina woman. "I know he means to do everything he can for us; but they make it hard for him, they won't let him." [16]

To many Americans, Roosevelt was more than a hero—he was almost a god. "We all feel if there ever was a saint, [Roosevelt] is one," a woman from Wiscon-

Governor Alf Landon

sin wrote in a letter to the president.[17] Another letter claimed that "as long as President Roosevelt will be our leader under Jesus Christ we will feel no fear."[18]

At the same time that he was admired and praised for his New Deal programs, Roosevelt was also treated by millions as a trusted old friend. From the first week of his presidency, Franklin and Eleanor Roosevelt received letters by the millions, asking advice for personal problems and offering opinions on the president's own affairs.

Most of the letters were from those hardest hit by the depression, asking for jobs or a little money to buy food for their families. Many letters were sad, touching reminders of how personal the depression was. "I am writing to see if you have any clothes that you could give me," a woman from Georgia wrote. "I live in the country, and I haven't got enough money. . . . I need a coat, if you have an old coat or sweater you can give me. . . . We have had a lot of bad luck."[19]

It was the people in need who clustered around Roosevelt in the election. For the first time in history, the votes of African Americans and labor were forces in an election. Although these were not the wealthy businessmen or the owners of newspapers, they *were* the majority.

And so it appeared to Franklin Roosevelt in 1936 that he had received what is called a mandate—a directive from the people telling him to forge ahead with his New Deal ideas. But oddly enough, it was this aggressive forging ahead that soon became troublesome for Roosevelt. It was a bad mistake to make, and it would, in a year or two, bring about the end of the New Deal.

Members of the Federal Theatre Project take control of the group's offices to protest the cutting of WPA jobs.

CHAPTER SIX

THE END OF THE NEW DEAL

"If [Roosevelt] were to say a kind word for the man-eating shark," stated an article in the *New York Times* after the election of 1936, "people would look thoughtful and say perhaps there *are* two sides to the question." [1]

Politically, the president must have felt almost invincible. It was, he decided, a good time to resolve some problems that had been troubling his New Deal for some time. The most troublesome, for Roosevelt, was the U.S. Supreme Court. If he was to go toe to toe with the Court, he would have no better time to do it than now, after his one-sided election win.

ROADBLOCKS TO THE NEW DEAL

The Supreme Court had thrown up several roadblocks to his New Deal legislation in 1935–1936. The first was in May 1935, when the Court decided that the NRA was unconstitutional. The federal government, which was regulating trade between and within states, was told by the Court that it could no longer be involved in trade within states. That was the jurisdiction of the state and local governments, said the Court, not the federal government.

In a similar ruling, the Supreme Court ruled that government could not become involved in setting minimum wage requirements—wage negotiations were between employers and workers.

Roosevelt's reaction was anger that "his mandate from the people and the bulging Democratic majorities in Congress could be neutralized by five old men on the Supreme Court." [2] He had realized that the NRA was not perfect, but he felt that it was a positive step toward getting the nation back to work.

The reaction of big business was far more positive—gleeful, in fact. No longer did business and industry have to bow to the demands of labor, a force growing

WPA actors rehearse for a performance.

Participants in a WPA program learn different ways to enjoy their leisure time.

stronger because of the NRA. With the Court ruling, businesses no longer had to abide by the NRA codes, and some of them could hardly wait to make it official. As one historian writes, ''The Hearst newspapers delightedly removed the Blue Eagle from their mastheads and ran American flags instead.''[3]

The Supreme Court dealt the New Deal an even more severe blow when it found another of Roosevelt's new agencies unconstitutional—the AAA. The Court objected to the tax that the federal government had imposed on those who processed the farmers' products. The purpose of the tax was to help the farmers, and it had seemed to be working—farm prices and farmers' incomes had risen almost 60 percent since the AAA began.

But the processors were upset that the tax was an unfair burden for them to carry. Many processors had gone bankrupt, and others warned that they, too, were financially strapped because of the tax. They brought the case to the Supreme Court, and won.

ROOSEVELT'S SOLUTION

The lawsuits against the NRA and the AAA were just the beginning. Legal actions against various New Deal agencies were piling up by the hundreds. Roosevelt and his staff worried that the Supreme Court was going to dismantle the New Deal piece by piece. He believed that something had to be done, and fast, or there would be nothing left of the Hundred Days legislation.

In February 1936 the president took on what he privately called the ''nine old men'' of the Supreme Court. He announced a plan which he said would ''reorganize'' the judicial system. According to the plan, for every justice who didn't retire at age 70, the president could appoint an additional justice. The new maximum for the Court would be 15, not 9.

Although his motives were clearly to get more liberal justices on the Court, ones who would vote pro-New Deal, Roosevelt made the plan sound less political. He insisted that the work load was heavy—far too much for nine men. He also referred to justices who sit on the bench of the Supreme Court ''in many instances far beyond their years of physical or mental capability.''[4]

Too, it was not as if the Court had never been reorganized. In fact, there had been many changes in the number of justices over the years. The Court had begun in 1789 with six, and had gone to five in 1801. The number had increased over the next 60 years to 10 in 1863, then had shrunk to 7 in 1866. The current number of 9 had been in place since 1869. Even so, the reaction to Roosevelt's plan was like tossing a match to gasoline. The Court was furious—in fact, Roosevelt biographer Ted Morgan writes, "there had not been such an insult to the Court since Theodore Roosevelt had described one of its members as 'an old fuzzy-wuzzy with sweetbread brains.'"[5]

And it was not only the Court that was outraged. In Congress there were many who spoke out against Roosevelt for being manipulative and underhanded. How could Roosevelt complain about justices who are too old, when 80-year-old Louis Brandeis was one of the most liberal of the Supreme Court justices? Clearly, this was a political move, not one to ease the Court's work load. Some in Congress who had previously backed the president were irritated and openly critical of Roosevelt's attempt at what they called "Court packing."

THE BEGINNING OF THE END

Roosevelt would not back down, however, and the Supreme Court issue was debated for months in Senate hearings. The controversy was never truly resolved. As Roosevelt and his supporters pressed for reorganization, the Court changed direction. In some unexpected decisions, the New Deal legislation was upheld, including the Social Security Act and the Wagner Act, a law that was Roosevelt's replacement for the now-dead NRA.

In addition to surprising Roosevelt with some liberal decisions, the Court went through some rapid personnel changes. Some conservative justices who had sat on the bench of the Supreme Court for many years decided to retire. This left vacancies that Roosevelt quickly filled with liberal-thinking appointees, and soon the Court was definitely more pro-New Deal. And even though the Senate hearings eventually struck down his reorganization plan, Roosevelt had come away with what he wanted. His programs were no longer in as much danger of being declared unconstitutional in the nation's highest court.

Even though Roosevelt "won" this war, however, historians are quick to point out that the Supreme Court affair was highly damaging politically to the president. Especially in Congress, the Court fight destroyed the unity of the Democratic party, Roosevelt's chief strength behind his New Deal reforms. Once a solid block backing the president, the Democrats in Congress were divided. As one historian remarks, "The new Court might be willing to uphold new laws, but a mutinous Congress would pass few of Roosevelt's measures for the justices to consider."[6]

"HIGH SCHOOL GIRL REVENGE"

After Roosevelt's controversial plan to reorganize the Supreme Court was voted down, the president was angry. He felt betrayed by many politicians, especially by Democrats who had opposed the plan. He stayed mad, too, at those who he privately called "deserters."

In the spirit of what one presidential critic called "high school girl revenge," Roosevelt and some close advisers came up with another idea. He felt that there was too much leeway in the term "Democrat," for, in addition to the liberal, New Deal Democrats, there were conservatives who more and more were opposing the New Deal.

Roosevelt proposed that only liberals be classified as Democrats, and only conservatives as Republicans. To purge the conservative Democrats from the party seemed like the most expedient way to strengthen the New Deal, Roosevelt thought. This purge could only happen if Americans voted the conservatives out of office, and the sooner the better. And to ensure that conservatives were voted out in 1938, Roosevelt proposed to campaign actively against the conservatives.

But there were some Roosevelt aides who felt that the president's involvement with such a plan was political suicide. James Farley, Roosevelt's campaign manager in the elections of 1932 and 1936, believed that the president would be risking a great deal by getting involved in state politics, and advised Roosevelt to abandon his plan. Roosevelt would not be dissuaded, however, and took to the campaign trail in 1938, working hard against conservative Democrats.

The results? Not far from what James Farley had predicted. As historian Don Lawson writes in *FDR's New Deal*, "[Roosevelt's] efforts succeeded only in making martyrs and easy winners out of almost everyone he opposed." In addition, there were additional, deeper splits between Congress and Roosevelt, making further New Deal legislation almost impossible.

OTHER SETBACKS

It was not the Court issue alone that ushered in the end of the New Deal. In the months that Roosevelt was taking on the Court, in business there was a great deal of strife between labor and management. Workers were organizing themselves into unions, and the unions were striking for higher salaries and increased benefits.

"SIT DOWN!"

One of the many criticisms leveled at Roosevelt and the New Deal was that it was too strict on business, making labor too powerful. Some of those fears worsened in late 1935 and 1936, when a rash of strikes occurred in the nation's largest automotive plants.

By today's standards, there seemed to be plenty of reasons for workers to be dissatisfied. Pay was low, work was sporadic, and the assembly lines moved too quickly. Workers who tried to organize unions were often threatened by management. In many factories, in fact, employers paid hundreds of thousands of dollars to detective agencies to spy on workers in order to determine whether a union was growing too powerful.

But these new strikes were quite different from previous ones. They were sit-down strikes. Not only did the workers stop working, they sat at their machines and refused to leave. The first was at a rubber plant in Akron, Ohio, but they soon spread to Michigan, where workers shut down several large automobile plants.

When management tried to drive the strikers out, they were assailed with showers of metal hinges, glass soda bottles, bolts, and coffee mugs. The governor of Michigan ordered that there be no violence, so the police and the National Guard could not use weapons.

The sit-down was effective, gaining strikers many demands throughout the late 1930s—much to the dismay of wealthy business owners.

Some of the strikes were violent, causing long delays in production and resulting in damage to factories. The strikes angered many Americans, who felt that labor had been given too much power by New Deal legislation. And many business leaders were furious with Roosevelt for refusing to use force to halt the strikes.

The president suffered another setback in 1937, when the economy began to falter. The number of unemployed workers rose from just under 5 million in the fall of 1937 to 11 million in May 1938. By 1938 one-sixth of New York City was on relief, and one-third of the city of Akron, Ohio. The stock market plunged crazily and profits plummeted. This time was called "Roosevelt's recession" by the president's growing numbers of opponents. America's middle class, once strongly behind the president, was quickly becoming edgy. Would every bit of ground they had gained since Roosevelt's New Deal began be lost?

A WPA road crew clearing project in Arkansas

Members of Eleanor Roosevelt's Reforestation Army line up for lunch.

Roosevelt strongly objected to comparisons of the recession of 1938 to Hoover's Great Depression. In his fireside chats he pointed out to Americans that their money was no longer in jeopardy, for the banks were safe. There were firmly rooted programs in place so that people did not have to worry about starving and becoming homeless.

In a message to Congress, Roosevelt said, "All we need today is to look upon the fundamental, sound economic conditions to know that this business recession causes more perplexity than fear on the part of most people, and to contrast our prevailing mental attitude with the terror and despair of five years ago." [7]

Roosevelt and his New Deal advisers took action against the recession, getting over $1 billion from Congress for relief and other programs to keep the economy from worsening. Even so, Roosevelt had lost his support in Congress. As Robert McElvaine writes, the problems Roosevelt had in his second term showed Congress that he could be beaten. "After leaving the New Deal once—and living to tell about it—it was much easier for a senator to oppose Roosevelt again." [8]

After 1938, Roosevelt was never able to win a single bit of reform legislation. "Dr. New Deal," as the president laughingly called his early administration, was finished.

ON OTHER FRONTS

The Great Depression, which had begun with the crash of the stock market in October 1929, had not ended with Roosevelt's New Deal. His decisive action during the Hundred Days did prevent what many economists say could have been complete and utter economic and social disaster in the United States. Millions of Americans were given relief, and millions more received jobs through various New Deal agencies.

On the negative side, when the New Deal came to an end, there were still eight million Americans out of work, and the economy was shaky. And critics of the New Deal maintain that Roosevelt's tactics of huge government spending to "prime the pump" of the economy created a dangerous trend that resulted in a monstrously high national debt that grows larger even today.

What finally ended the depression and brought back record-high employment figures was not an internal force but an external one. As Roosevelt sparred with the Court, as labor and management were screaming at each other, as Congress was digging in its heels and refusing to cooperate with the president, thunderclouds were gathering in Europe. Rumblings of war in Europe, beginning with a German nation led by a new power-hungry dictator named Adolf Hitler, were gradually being heard in the United States.

It was the preparation for battle that would end the depression. All who wanted employment would have jobs, and profits would soar. The way out of the worst economic nightmare in American history turned out to be the way to war.

Four young Civilian Conservation Corps members clear a path for a highway.

SOURCE NOTES

INTRODUCTION

1. FDR quoted in Rebecca Larsen, *Franklin D. Roosevelt: Man of Destiny* (New York: Franklin Watts, 1991), 104.

2. Quoted in Robert S. McElvaine, *The Great Depression* (New York: Times Books, 1984), 130.

3. Edmund Wilson quoted in William Leuchtenburg, *The New Deal and War* (New York: Time-Life Books, 1964), 8.

4. FDR quoted in Don Lawson, *FDR's New Deal* (New York: Thomas Y. Crowell, 1979), 24.

CHAPTER ONE

1. Quoted in Lawson, 24.

2. Bruce Glassman, *The Crash of '29 and the New Deal* (Morristown, New Jersey: Silver Burdett, 1986), 15.

3. Coolidge quoted in McElvaine, 16.

4. Ibid., 14.

5. Hoover quoted in Milton Meltzer, *Brother, Can You Spare a Dime?* (New York: Alfred A. Knopf, 1969), 5.

6. Quoted in McElvaine, 17.

7. Sam G. Johnson, personal interview, May 5, 1992.

8. Anne E. Schraff, *The Great Depression and the New Deal* (New York: Franklin Watts, 1990), 13.

9. John Raskob quoted in Dixon Wecter, *The Age of the Great Depression* (New York: Macmillan, 1948), 4.

10. Schraff, 17.

11. Quoted in Meltzer, 10.

CHAPTER TWO

1. Quoted in Meltzer, 11.

2. Ibid., 11.

3. Chester Johnson, personal interview, May 5, 1992.

4. Hoover quoted in Lawson, 13.

5. Quoted in Charles Jellison, *Tomatoes Were Cheaper: Tales from the Thirties* (Syracuse, New York: Syracuse University Press, 1977), 14.

6. Robert Bendiner, *Just Around the Corner: A Highly Selective History of the Thirties* (New York: E.P. Dutton, 1967), 4.

7. Meltzer, 69.

8. Schraff, 24.

9. Chester Johnson, personal interview, May 5, 1992.

10. Wecter, 18.

11. Quoted in William Hull, *The Dirty Thirties* (Minneapolis: Stanton Publishers, 1989), 20.

12. Quoted in Meltzer, 87.

CHAPTER THREE

1. Quoted in Anthony J. Badger, *The New Deal: The Depression Years* (New York: Hill and Wang, 1989), 41.

2. Schraff, 22.

3. Quoted in McElvaine, 52.

4. Quoted in Schraff, 22.

5. Bendiner, 10.

6. Frederick Allen, *Since Yesterday: The 1930s in America* (New York: Harper and Row, 1939), 84.

7. Allen, 85.

8. McElvaine, 94.

9. Quoted in Glassman, 35.

10. McElvaine, 94.

11. Bendiner, 25.

12. Schraff, 64.

13. Larsen, 67.

14. Quoted in Schraff, 43.

15. Larsen, 86.

16. Schraff, 44.

17. Meltzer, 115.

CHAPTER FOUR
1. Allen, 97.
2. Kenneth Davis, *FDR: The New Deal Years 1933–1937* (New York: Random House, 1979), 28.
3. Quoted in Lawson, 41.
4. Quoted in Leuchtenburg, 10.
5. Allen, 109–110.
6. Davis, 60.
7. Bendiner, 34.
8. Quoted in Lawson, 48.
9. Quoted in Davis, 63.
10. Miles Van Horner, personal interview, May 13, 1992.
11. Larsen, 112.
12. Quoted in McElvaine, 152.
13. Ibid., 152.
14. Hull, 125.
15. John Steinbeck, *The Grapes of Wrath* (New York: Viking Press, 1939), 88.
16. Larsen, 116.
17. Quoted in McElvaine, 156.
18. Quoted in Leuchtenburg, 14.
19. Bendiner, 41.

CHAPTER FIVE
1. Allen, 217.
2. Ibid., 231.
3. McElvaine, 160.
4. Bendiner, 69.
5. Leuchtenburg, 51.
6. Bendiner, 134.
7. McElvaine, 238.
8. Ibid., 238.
9. Ibid., 239.
10. Allen, 187.
11. Rita James Simon, *As We Saw the Thirties* (Urbana, Ill.: University of Illinois Press, 1967), 111.
12. Lawson, 108.
13. McElvaine, 257.

14. Quoted in McElvaine, 279.

15. Dorothy Thompson quoted in McElvaine, 281.

16. Robert McElvaine, ed., *Down & Out in the Great Depression: Letters from the Forgotten Man* (Chapel Hill, North Carolina: University of North Carolina Press, 1983), 113.

17. Ibid., 14.

18. Ibid.

19. Ibid., 76–77.

CHAPTER SIX

1. *New York Times,* Dec. 4, 1936, quoted in Leuchtenburg, 67.

2. McElvaine, 283.

3. Leuchtenburg, 68.

4. Allen, 296.

5. Ted Morgan, *FDR: A Biography* (New York: Simon and Schuster, 1985), 470.

6. Leuchtenburg, 71.

7. Quoted in Leuchtenburg, 74.

8. McElvaine, 286.

FOR FURTHER READING

Allen, Frederick Lewis. *Since Yesterday: The 1930s in America*. New York: Harper and Row, 1939.

Badger, Anthony J. *The New Deal: The Depression Years, 1933–1940*. New York: Hill and Wang, 1989.

Bendiner, Robert. *Just Around the Corner: A Highly Selective History of the Thirties*. New York: E.P. Dutton, 1967.

Glassman, Bruce. *The Crash of '29 and The New Deal*. Morristown, New Jersey: Silver Burdett, 1986.

Hull, William H. *The Dirty Thirties*. Edina, Minn.: Wm. H. Hull, 1989.

Jellison, Charles. *Tomatoes Were Cheaper: Tales from the Thirties*. Syracuse, New York: Syracuse University Press, 1977.

Larsen, Rebecca. *Franklin D. Roosevelt: Man of Destiny*. New York: Franklin Watts, 1991.

Lawson, Don. *FDR's New Deal*. New York: Thomas Y. Crowell, 1979.

McElvaine, Robert S. *Down & Out in the Great Depression*. Chapel Hill, North Carolina: University of North Carolina Press, 1983.

———. *The Great Depression*. New York: Times Books, 1984.

Meltzer, Milton. *Brother, Can You Spare a Dime?* New York: Alfred A. Knopf, 1969.

Morgan, Ted. *FDR: A Biography*. New York: Simon and Schuster, 1985.

Schraff, Anne E. *The Great Depression and the New Deal*. New York: Franklin Watts, 1990.

Shebar, Sharon. *Franklin D. Roosevelt and the New Deal*. Chicago: Childrens Press, 1987.

Simon, Rita James. *As We Saw the Thirties*. Urbana, Ill: University of Illinois Press, 1967.

Wecter, Dixon. *The Age of the Great Depression*. New York: Macmillan, 1948.

INDEX

A

African Americans, 87, 89
Agricultural Adjustment Act (AAA),
    70–72, 93
alcohol, 66–67
anti-Semitism, 84
apple sellers, *26ill, 38, 39ill*
army, the, 49, 68–70
automobile industry, 15, 16, 96

B

bank holidays, 59–60, 63–64, 66
banks, *29ill,* 45–46, 59–60, 63–64,
    66, 77–80, 83–84
    and stock market, 17, 19–20, 25,
    27, 28
Black Thursday, 20, *22ill, 23ill,
    24ill,* 25
Bonus Army March 1932, *42ill,* 46–
    50, *47ill, 48ill, 50ill, 51ill*
    1933, 79
Brain Trust, The, 67, 74, 77, 79, 87
breadlines, 34-37, *36ill*
business and industry, 14–17, 27–
    28, 32–33, 64, 77–80, 95–
    96. *See also* stock market

and NRA, 74, 91–93

C

campaigns, political, 54–56, *55ill,*
    82, 87–88, 95
charity, 45, 87. *See also* relief pro-
    grams
children, 33, 37
    labor regulations for, 74, 80
Chrysler, Walter, 16
Civilian Conservation Corps (CCC),
    68–70, *69ill,* 79, *92ill, 97ill,
    99ill*
communism, 67, 79–80, 82. *See also*
    socialism
Congress, 15, 46–49, 98
    and New Deal legislation, 67, 72
    and Roosevelt, 63, 75, 94, 95
Coolidge, Calvin, 15–16
Coughlin, Father Charles Edward,
    83–84, *84ill*
credit, 16–18, 45–46
criticism
    of Hoover, 46, 50, 59–60
    of New Deal, 75, 77–86, 87, 96,
    98

PHOTOGRAPHIC ACKNOWLEDGMENTS

Cover photographs courtesy of The Bettmann Archive and the FDR Library

All interior photographs courtesy of The Bettmann Archive

On the cover: (*Upper Left*) A line extends around the block for a 1¢ restaurant. (*Upper Right*) An unemployed man sells apples on a New York street. (*Lower Right*) Ranks of ''Dollar a Day'' men march through the streets with signs showing the skills they have to offer. (*Lower Left*) Depression-era children wait in camps for their fathers, who are lobbying in Congress for veteran's affairs. (*Back*) Unemployed single women protest the hiring of married women in Boston.

On the title page: Throngs of unemployed men wait in line outside the Municipal Lodging House in New York for Sunday dinner.

ABOUT THE AUTHOR

Gail Stewart is the author of more than 60 books for children and young adults. A former junior-high English teacher, she earned her B.A. at Gustavus Adolphus College. She did her graduate work in linguistics, Old English, and curriculum study at the College of St. Thomas and the University of Minnesota. An avid reader and tennis player, she lives in Minneapolis, Minnesota, with her husband and their three sons.